Guide for Romanian and German Labour Law
Basics of the Employment Relationship

by

Carmen NENU
Carmina POPESCU
Ilona ZENKER

NENU Carmen, born 1968, studied at the University of Bucharest/Romania and graduated with a P.hD. in Law and with a Master degree in European Public Affairs Management.
After serving as a legal adviser and deputy chief for labor-law related public institutions since 1994, and after working as a lawyer, since 2000 she teaches her deeply profound theoretical and practical knowledge, experienced in countless cases, as a lecturer at University.
From 1997 to 2007 she was President of an NGO with social purposes. Beside that, she is also member of various Law Associations and author of dozens of articles and studies in the field of labor-law and labor-law related issues.

POPESCU Carmina, born 1981, studied at the University of Bucharest/Romania and graduated with a P.hD. in Law and with a Master degree in Public Administration.
Since 2004 she is constantly engaged in Romanian Labour Law, Social Security Law and Familiy Law. She is (founding-) member of various Law and Administration associations and has as a (co-) author published dozens of studies in national and international specialised journals. She teaches her deeply profound theoretical and practical knowledge, experienced in countless cases, as a lecturer at University.

ZENKER Ilona, born 1965, studied at the University of Augsburg/Germany Law including special finance- and business-administration sciences, and graduated with a P.hD. in Law.
After serving as a lawyer at court and in public service, since 1994 she is self-employed as a (founding-) executive partner of a law firm, specialised in counselling and representing private owned (international) companies as well as public corporations and trusts. From the beginning in 1994 she is permanently practising the full scale of German Labour Law. She is also Member of various Law associations and teaches her deeply profound theoretical and practical knowledge, experienced in countless cases, as a lecturer at University.

Herstellung und Verlag
BoD – Books on Demand, Norderstedt
ISBN 978-3-7357-7857-4

Romanian and German Labour Law

Guide for Romanian and German Labour Law
Basics of the Employment Relationship

List of Abbreviations

AG	Aktiengesellschaft (public limited company, stock corporation)
AGG	Allgemeines Gleichbehandlungsgesetz (Act on Equal Treatment)
ArbG	Arbeitsgericht (Labour Court of first Instance)
ArbGG	Arbeitsgerichtsgesetz (Act on Court Procedure in Labour Law)
ArbNErfG	Arbeitsnehmererfindungsgesetz (Employee Invention Act)
ArbPlSchG	Arbeitsplatzschutzgesetz (Act on Protect of the Workplace)
ArbSchG	Arbeitsschutzgesetz (Occupational Safety and Health Act)
ArbZG	Arbeitsgesetz (Act on Working Time)
art.	article
Aufenthg	Aufenthaltsgesetz (Act on Residence)
AÜG	Arbeitnehmerüberlassungsgesetz (Act on Commercial Temporary Work and Commercial Transfer of Employees)
BAG	Bundesarbeitsgericht (Federal Labour Court)
BBG	Bundesbeamtengesetz (Civil Service Law)
BBiG	Berufsbildungsgesetz (Occupational Training Act)
BDSG	Bundesdatenschutzgesetz (Federal Data Protection Act)
BEEG	Bundeselterngeld- und Elternzeitgesetz (Act on Parental Leave and Parental Time)
BeschFG	Beschäftigungsförderungsgesetz (Act on the Improvement of Employment Opportunities)
BetrVG	Betriebsverfassungsgesetz (Works Constitution Act)
BGB	Bürgerlisches Gesetzbuch (Civil Code)
BGH	Bundesgerichtshof (Federal Court of Justice)
BUrlG	Bundesurlaubsgesetz (Federal Vacation Act)
BVerfG	Bundesverfassungsgericht (Supreme Constitutional Court)

Guide for Romanian and German Labour Law
Basics of the Employment Relationship

CDU	Christliche-Demokratische Union (Christian Democratic Union)
CEEP	European Centre of Enterprises with Public Participation
CSU	Christliche-Soziale Union (Christian Social Union)
EC	European Commission
ECJ	Europäischer Gerichtshof (European Court of Justice)
ed.	edition
EEC	European Economic Community
EFZG	Entgeltfortzahlungsgesetz (Act on Continued Payment of Remuneration on Holidays and in Case of Sickness)
e.g.	exempli gratia
EGBGB	Einführungsgesetz zum bürgerlichen Gesetzbuch (Introductory Act of German Civil Code)
EU	Europäische Union (European Union)
et seq.	et sequitur
ETUC	European Trade Union Confederation
EuGH	Europäischer Gerichtshof (European Court of Justice)
GDR	Deutsche Demokratische Republik, DDR (German Democratic Repuplic)
GewO	Gewerbeordnung (Trade Regulation Act)
GG	Grundgesetz (Constitution)
GKG	Gerichtskostengesetz (Court Fees Act)
GmbH	Gesellschaft mit beschränkter Haftung (Company with limited liabilty)
HAG	Heimarbeitsgesetz (Act on Homework)
HGB	Handelsgesetzbuch (Commercial Code)
IAO	Internationale Arbeitsorganisation (International Labour Organisation)
ILO	International Labour Organisation
InsO	Insolvenzordnung (Insolvency Act)
JArbSchG	Jugendarbeitsschutzgesetz (Young Person Employment Act)
KG	Kommanditgesellschaft (Limited commercial partnership)
KSchG	Kündigungsschutzgesetz (Dismissal Protection Act or Law of Protection against Unlawful Dismissal)

Guide for Romanian and German Labour Law
Basics of the Employment Relationship

LAG	Landesarbeitsgesetz (Land Labour Court)
MindArbBedG	Gesetz über Mindestarbeitsbedingungen (Act on Minimum Working Conditions)
MuSchG	Mutterschutzgesetz (Maternity Protection Act)
NachwG	Nachweisgesetz (Law of Notification of Conditions)
NGO	Non-guvernamental Organisations
no.	number
NZA	Neue Zeitschrift für Arbeits- und Sozialrecht
OHG	Offene Handelsgesellschaft (general partnership)
p.	page
para.	paragraph
RichterG	Richtergesetz (Judicary Act)
SchwbG	Schwerbehindertengesetz (Act on Disabled Persons)
SGB	Sozialgesetzbuch (Social Security Code)
SPD	Sozialdemokratische Partei Deutschlands (Social Democratic Party)
TVG	Tarifvertragsgesetz (Act on Collective Agreements)
TzBfG	Teilzeit- und Befristungsgesetz (Act on Part-Time Work and Fixed-Term Contracts)
UNICE	Industry and Employers Confederations of Europe
UWG	Gesetz gegen unlauteren Wettbewerb (Act against Unfair Competition)
Vol	volume
WRV	Weimarer Reichsverfassung (Weimar Constitution)

TABLE of CONTENTS

Prologue

Part 1 – Romanian Labour Law

Title I
General Considerations On The Individual Work Contract

Title II
Conclusion Of The Individual Work Contract

1.　　The legal capacity of the person to be employed
　　a)　　Incompatibilities
　　b)　　Concurrent positions
2.　　Legal capacity of the employer
　　a)　　The legal entity employer
　　b)　　The individual employer
3.　　Limitations of the legal capacity of individuals to individual
　　employment contracts as an employer

II.　Consent of the parties on concluding the individual labor contract

III.　The subject and cause of the individual labor contract

IV.　The form of the individual employment contract

Chapter 2
Specific conditions necessary for the valid conclusion of the individual labor contract

I.　The medical examination

II.　Checking personal skills and professional training of individuals applying for employment

III.　Approval, work permit and commitment

IV.　Probation

V.　Education and work experience conditions

Title III
Rights And Obligations Of The Parties Of The Individual Employment Contract

Chapter 1
Contents of the individual employment contract

I.　The non-compete clause

II.　The mobility clause

III.　The confidentiality clause

IV.　The clause on training

Chapter 2
The basic rights of the employer and the employee

I.　The employer's right to organize the work of the firm

II.   The right of the employer to issue directives regarding the employee activity

III. The employer's right to control the employee's work, to find and punish misbehavior

IV.   The employee's right to receive wages

Title IV
Modification, Suspension And Termination Of The Individual Employment Contract

Chapter 1
Changing the individual employment contract

I.   Modification by agreement of the parties

II.   Unilateral modification of the individual employment contract initiated by the employer
   1.   Delegation
   2.   Job relocation

Chapter 2
Suspension of the individual employment contract

I.   Suspension de jure of the individual employment contract

II.   Suspension of the individual employment contract by agreement of the parties

III. Suspension of the individual employment contract on the initiative of the employer

IV.   Suspension of the individual employment contract on the employee's initiative

Chapter 3
Termination of the individual employment contract

I.   Termination de jure of the individual employment contract

II.   Termination of the individual employment contract by the agreement of the parties

III. Resignation - termination of the individual employment contract on the employee's unilateral initiative

IV.   Dismissal - termination of the employment contract on the employer's initiative
   1.   The dismissal for reasons related to the person of the employee
   2.   Dismissal for reasons unrelated to the employee
   3.   Collective dismissal

Title V
Types Of Individual Employment Contracts

I. **The typical individual employment contract**
1. Indefinite duration
2. Full time employment
3. The work place

II. **The individual fixed-term employment contract**
1. The national regulation of the individual employment contract of limited duration
2. Community legislation of the individual fixed-term employment

III. **The individual part-time employment contract**
1. Regulation of the individual part-time employment contract in law
2. Regulation of the part-time individual employment contract by Community law

IV. **The individual work at home contract**
1. Internal regulations on work at home contracts
2. Community concerns related to work at home contracts

V. **Work through a temporary employment agency**
1. Internal regulations on work through a temporary employment agency
2. EU regulations on work through a temporary employment agency

VI. **The on-the-job apprenticeship contract**
1. The internal regulation of the on-the-job apprenticeship contract.
2. Community legislation for on-the-job apprenticeship Contracts

Title VI
Individual labour disputes and work jurisdiction

I. **Individual labour disputes**
II. **Labour jurisdiction**
1. The panel of judges
2. Material and territorial competence of the courts
   a) Material competence
   b) Territorial jurisdiction
3. Deadlines for courts referral
4. Appeal
5. Stamp duty

Part 2 – German Labour Law

Foreword

Title I
General Consideration of the Individual Employment Contract

Chapter 1

I. **In General**
1. Conditions of an Individual Employment Contract
2. Distinctions and other Types of Contract
3. Contract Parties
    a. Employees
        - Employee-like persons
        - Executive Staff
        - Freelance Collaborators
        - Civil Servants
    b. Employer

II. **Theories about the sources of individual employment relationship**
1. Integration Theory
2. Contract Theory

Chapter 2
Sources of German Labour Law
and Employment Relationship

I. **Law of Nations / International Law / Law of EU**
1. Law of Nations
    a. International Labour Organisation (IAO)
    b. European Convention of Human Rights and European Social Charter
2. International Law
3. Law of the European Union

II. **National Law**
1. Hierarchy of sources of German Labour Law and the Employment Relationship
2. Constitution
3. Ordinary Legislation
4. Court Decisions
5. Employment Contract
6. Collective Agreements
7. Company Agreements
8. General Terms and Conditions

9.   Custom
10.   Right to Issue Instructions
11.   Overview of the ranking

Title II
General Conditions for the Conclusion of an Individual Employment Contract

Chapter 1

I.   Legal capacity
    1.   Legal incapacity
    2.   Limited legal capacity
    3.   under-age employees and employers

II.   Legal prohibitions of concluding an employment contract

III.   Formal requirement
    1.   General formal provisions
    2.   Law on notification of conditions governing an employment relationship – Nachweisgesetz

IV.   Agreement by consensus on the employment contract

V.   Power of an attorney and proxy
    1.   Authority by law and by power of an attorney
    2.   Representation with power of an attorney
    3.   Representation without power of an attorny

Chapter 2
The Hiring Process

I.   Job Advertising
    1.   „Invitatio ad offerendum"
    2.   General Equal Treatment Act
        a.   in general
        b.   legal consequences

II.   Application
    1.   Duties of Revelation
    2.   Legal consequences

III.   Job interview
    1.   Right to ask question
        a.   Pregnancy
        b.   Physical Disability
        c.   Conviction
        d.   Age
        e.   HIV Infection
        f.   Employee of the State security service of the GDR
    2.   Tests and medical examination
    3.   Further sources of information
    4.   Reimbursement of expenses and so forth

Chapter 3
Faults of the employment contract

I. **Causes of nullity**
   1. Section 134 of the German Civil Code (BGB)
   2. Section 138 of the German Civil Code (BGB)

II. **Causes of rescission**
   1. Section 119 paragraph II of the German Civil Code (BGB)
   2. Section 123 of the German Civil Code (BGB)

III. **Legal consequences**

Title III
Legal relationship – Rights and Duties of employer and employee

Chapter 1

I. **Right of the employer and corresponding duties of the employees**

   1. Right of the employer to organize the work – Duty of the employee to work
   2. Right of the employer to issue directions – Duty of the employee to follow directions
   3. Right of the employer to control – Personal right of the employee
   4. Right of the employer to demand loyalty and other duties of behaviour
   5. Right of the employer to demand confidentiality
   6. Right of the employer to prohibit competition

II. **Duties of the employers and corresponding rights of the employees**
   1. Duty to grant holiday
   2. Duty to pay remuneration
   a. Different types of wages
   b. Overtime hours
   c. Work on Sundays, Public Holidays an Night work
   d. Short-time work
   3. Futher duties

Chapter 2
Payment without work

I. **Annual holiday, sick leave, maternity**

II. **Employee`s absence of short duration**

III. **Default of acceptance of the employer**

IV. **Employer´s risk**

Title IV
Modification, suspension and termination of the individual employment contract

Chapter 1
Termination by mutual consent

Chapter 2
Termination by extraordinary and ordinary dismissal

I. **Extraordinary Dismissal**

II. **Ordinary Dismissal**
1.) Dismissals on grounds of personal capability
2.) Dismissals on grounds of conduct
3.) Termination for operational reasons

III. **Special Case**
Dismissal with the option of altered conditions of employment

Chapter 3
Other reasons for Termination

I. **Rescission of contract**

II. **Expiry of a period**

III. **Death of the employee**

IV. **Voluntary Service in the Army**

V. **Reaching the age limit**

Chapter 4
Unlawful Reasons for Termination

I.   **Transfer of the company**

II.   **Business Cessation and Company Insolvency**
1.)   Business Cessation
2.)   Company Insolvency

III.   **Basic Miltary Service**

IV.   **Death of the Employer**

Title V

Chapter 1
Freedom of Contract

Chapter 2
Various Types of Individual Labour Contract

I.   **Full-Time Contract for an indefinite Period**

II.   **Contract for a definite Period**

III.   **Contract for part-time Work**

IV.   **Contract for temporary Labour**

V.   **Contract tor marginal Employment / Mini-jobs**

VI.   **Homework / Telework**

VII.   **Employment / On-Call Work**

VIII.   **Job-Sharing**

Title VI
Jurisdicition

Chapter 1
System of Labour Courts

Chapter 2
Organs of Judicature

I.   **Professional Judge**

II.   **Lay Judge**

III.   **Lawyers and other Representatives**

Guide for Romanian and German Labour Law
Basics of the Employment Relationship

Chapter 3
Procedural Principles

I. **Venue and subject-matter jurisdiction**

II. **Procedure**

III. **Appeal**

IV. **Costs**

Chapter 4
Everday Business at Court

I. **Indemnity**

II. **Employment reference**

Prologue

The cultural relationship between Germany and Romania goes back a long way.

As early as 1714 Dimitrie Cantemir was a member of the German "Berliner Akademie," and at the beginning of the 19th century the Romanian writer I. Budai-Deleanu compiled (the first?) German - Romanian dictionary.

Since 1989 several cultural treaties have intensified the friendly and fruitful co-operation between the two countries and the number of school and university partnerships is increasing continuously.

The Friendship Treaty of 1992 forged close political ties and the opening of the (Romanian?) Chamber of Industry and Commerce in September 2002 further promoted the bilateral economical relationship.

The basis of successful economical cooperation between countries is first and foremost the collaboration between companies of both countries. However, every company depends crucially on a relationship of mutual trust between employers and employees. The employees are always the last link in a long chain and their work force is a decisive factor in a well-functioning market. Europe is increasingly growing together, as is the economical relationship between Germany and Romania and their relevant companies, exemplified by the progressive exchange of goods and personnel. It is therefore essential to understand the smallest nucleus of this relationship, the nucleus which keeps the companies in both countries running, namely the employment relationship between employees and employers.

This book provides an outline of German and Romanian Labour Laws and hopes to improve the mutual understanding of the legal system of each country, in particular regarding the legal relationship between employees and employers. Gaining a deeper insight into the legal framework of the other country is a further step towards growing together into a strong European Union which is indeed united in all respects.

Part 1
Romanian Labour Law

Title I
General Considerations On The Individual Work Contract

Chapter 1
The Evolution Of Legal Regulation Of Individual Employment Relationship

I.   Work and its types. Concept and Object of the legal Employment Relationship

Work, as a conscious and necessary human activity in the nature control and change process, takes place in society as a social relationship.

Employment is done in a democratic state under the competence criterion that provides paid employment. Thus, it is only able to ensure effective and efficient development of society.

Work performed is not always the object of legal relations of employment. There are a number of situations in which work leads to the creation of other legal relationships, not covered by the central institution of labor law - the individual employment contract.

Thus, relationships that arise between the school and students, or between higher education institutions and students, including periods of practice, are not based on the individual employment contract.

Also, a traditional legal work relationship does not exist between the service provider and the beneficiary, which are parts of a civil contract, between the agent and the principal or between the client and provider of a liberal profession.

In the legal work relationship the person involved in it provides a continuing activity by repeated use of their workforce. In this repeated process, skills, training, personal skills of the person providing work are particularly important and make representation unacceptable.

Work may not be performed in all conditions. The essence of the legal work is subordination of an employee to their employer. It is a specific subordination, involving employment in an organization, a certain organizational structure and some functional hierarchy.

Subordination has many aspects, among which the most important implies for the employee compliance with work discipline, with its basic component - respecting the working hours. Work discipline is an objective condition, it is necessary and indispensable to carrying out the activity in compliance with each employer. Corollary of this obligation of the employee, the employer is entitled to issue mandatory instructions to the employee, under the obligation to pay the employees.

It should be noted that this is not a total subordination, a waiver of employee rights and fundamental freedoms.

In order to contribute decisively to the creation of employment relationship, the provision of a work activity must have an outcome. This means obtaining an income in the form of a salary. Thus, the aim of the employee, for whom an individual work contract is established, is reached. This aim is to obtain the means of existence. No voluntary work can be subject to the individual employment contract.

Employment legal relationships are defined in the literature as those social relations regulated by law that arise between individuals, they are also defined as a legal rule, that follows the provision of some work by the first person for the benefit of the second, The beneficiary must pay for the work provided and create the conditions necessary for the provision of that work[1].

Relationships between the legal parties work usually develop according to the law. However, there are cases when disagreements between employers and employees are born. In these cases, either part of the legal employment relationship may be bound by coercive measures, established by the competent courts, to solve these conflicts of rights. They have to respect the obligations that they violated intentionally or unintentionally[2].

II.   Theories about the source of legal work

The individual employment relationship has certain features. Some are shared with other legal relationships, not covered by labor law and others are specific, distinctive, and define and individualize it as a legal institution. Thus, the legal individual employment relationship has the following characteristics:

---

[1] S. Ghimpu, I.T. Stefănescu, Ş. Beligrădeanu, G. Mohanu, Tratat de dreptul muncii, vol. 1, Editura ştiinţifică şi enciclopedică, Bucureşti, 1978, p. 8-9; S. Ghimpu, Al. Ţiclea, Dreptul muncii, 2 nd ed., All Beck Publishing House, Bucureşti, 2002, p. 16
[2] M. Volonciu, Totul despre conflictele de drepturi în relaţia salariat angajator, in „Adevărul Economic" no. 13/2001, p. 21

a. It is created only between two people, unlike other legal obligation relationships, where there may be a plurality of active or passive subjects;

b. One side of the legal work relationship is always an individual person, excluding creation of the legal work relationship between two legal entities;

c. It is concluded intuitu ending persons, considering the training, skills and qualities of the person who works, as well as employer characteristics, its organizational culture and working conditions offered;

d. A special relationship of legal subordination is born between the work provider and the beneficiary;

e. The object of the legal work relationship is represented by the main interdependent obligations of the parties, that is, work performed by the employee and payment of wages by the employer;

f. It is governed by the principle of protection of employee rights, as a feature of the constitutional principle of proportionality. According to this principle any restriction of rights must be justified by an interest.

The analysis of the Labour Code provisions shows that the legal work relationships mainly arise as a result of concluding an individual employment contract, which does not exclude the possibility that they also have other sources, complementary to the legal act or even completely independent of it.

II.1.   Non-contractual theories

Non-contractual theories mainly state that the legal individual employment relationship does not have its source in a contract. Its source lies both in professional statutes, that is, in the provider's effective integration into the functional hi-

erarchy of a legal entity and in the effective provision of labor, as a manifestation of will materialized in deeds and not
in legal documents. Within these conceptions the legal work
relationship has its source primarily in law and in professional
status on the one hand, and in the institutional organization
on the other hand.

Historical development of legal employment relationships of
civil servants and of other professional groups shows that these relationships have their source mainly in professional statutes, being distinct from other legal work relationships. These
professionals have to serve the public interest. They have a
legal individual work relationship with a special character as
compared to classical employees who are protected by the
rules of labor law. It is true that in the case of these legal relationships the will of the two sides to create an individual
employment relationship is involved. But the way the legal
will is expressed is regulated by law, by professional statutes
and not by the concluding a bilateral legal act.

We can say that administrative law has created a distinct individual employment relationship, different from the classic
legal source, meeting the objectives of this branch of law.

Thus, in Romania, as in other European countries, boundaries
have been defined between the legal labor relations of
those who hold an office of public power and legal labor relations arising by signing individual contracts of employment.
Another theory, mainly supported by German scholars, fol-
lowers of the employment relationship governed by law, fo-
cuses on integrating the employee in the working team. This
team is established within the company as a legal entity, as
a hierarchically organized whole, a combination of material
and human well-structured resources with a common goal.

According to this theory, freedom of work does not manifest itself according to its valences. Particular interests are overshadowed by the group interest, by the common interest of the legal entity employing. The employment relationship is governed only by law and by the institutional framework of the employer and does not have its source in a legal act.

II.2. Contractualist theories

Throughout the historical development of the individual employment relationship, the contractual grounding concept has seen different versions, from the theory of the exchange contract to the adhesion contract theory, theories which will be summarized below.

a. The exchange contract theory

At the beginning of the industrial revolution, the individual employment relationship was contractually conceived as an exchange of providing work for payment. Based on this bilateral mechanism, the legal work relationship is created individually, enjoying legal recognition that generally provides binding to the agreement.

Viewed from another perspective, however, the legal contract of employment based on the contract of exchanging salary for work performed, highlights a conflict between employer and employee. Thus, the employer's interest is to constantly reduce production costs. These costs include living labor costs, that is, salaries, obviously opposing the interest of the employee. Moreover, the contract is only a legal point of intersection of the two sides' wills, which basically differ in terms of purpose of concluding the legal act.

The only flaw of this contractual concept is that it fails to regard workforce as intrinsic to the human being, that is, to the worker. Thus, the worker cannot be treated as an ordinary commodity, because it can not be separated from the consumer in the work process.

Due to the fact that workforce has a character that is intrinsic to the human nature, the idea of clarifying it as not belonging to the category of goods was imposed forcefully.

Consequently, according to the ILO Constitution " work is not a commodity ", having the following distinctive features of the concept of commodity[3]:

- It is inseparable from the individual that provides it;

- It is impossible to be preserved, as it is consumed and created on a continuous basis;

- It is impossible to increase its amount without affecting the health of the person providing it.

This actual contractualist view of the legal work relationship based on the exchange of work performed and salary is still maintained. However, it is to be mentioned that this qualification of the individual employment contract as a contract of exchange does not have its meaning in the civil law, that is, that of exchanging things[4].

b.   The theory of adhesion contract

According to this theory, the employee is free to join the predisposition of the employer to provide a certain work, un-

---

[3] See, in this regard, I.T. Ștefănescu, Tratat de dreptul muncii, Wolters Kluwer Publishing House, București, 2007, p.12-13
[4] I.T. Ștefănescu, Tratat de dreptul muncii, Wolters Kluwer Publishing House, București, 2007, p. 190

der certain circumstances[5]. The employment relationship is actually created on a "diktat" imposed by one party, namely the one that is dominant in the execution of the legal work. The argument of supporters of this concept lies in the fact that, in order to have an individual employment contract, this does not necessarily have to be the result of negotiations on different terms.

It it is sufficient if a party would adhere to conditions imposed by the other party. The employee consents to an individual employment relationship as the result of formal freedom and equality between the two parties when concluding the individual employment contract. However, these circumstances are not covered by legal rules governing the freedom of contract.

c.   The theory of associative contract

This theory states that there is an unusual combination between employer and employee, based on the existence of a common purpose, function of the common overriding interests[6]. The theory can not be sustained because the two sides of the individual employment contract can not have absolutely common interests. Their legal willingness intersects at the time the individual employment contract is concluded, but their purpose is essentially different. The employee has a general obligation of fidelity and loyalty to the employer.

In the labor legislation of our country the rule, usually resulting from the analysis of the Labour Code provisions, is that the individual employment legal relationships are born by

---

[5] I.T. Ştefănescu, Tratat de dreptul muncii, Wolters Kluwer Publishing, Bucureşti, 2007, p. 191
[6] I.T. Ştefănescu, Tratat de dreptul muncii, Wolters Kluwer Publishing, Bucureşti, 2007, p. 191

concluding the individual employment contract. As an exception, legal work relationships can also arise according to
the regulations of special laws, mainly for professional groups
exercising their powers under the law and under professional
statutes.

CHAPTER 2
Individual Employment Contract - Concept and Importance

**I.   The individual employment contract - place and
importance in the legal sources of law of individual
employment relationships.**

The legal work relationship is performed for long periods,
usually during the active life, taking effect in the periods in
which the former provider withdraws from the active life, following the occurrence of social risks.

The importance of these legal relations should be considered
not only in terms of numbers, but also in terms of the intrinsic
relationship between workforce and human personality.
There is a multitude of internal and international regulations
and occupational statutes, of collective agreements governing the conclusion, execution, amendment, suspension and
termination of legal work relationships. Thus, the legal labor
relationship finds its regulation firstly in the fundamental law
that establishes social security rights of employees. Secondly,
it is regulated by the Labor Code, as the general law governing legal relations of both the individual and collective work
and the ones related to them. Finally, the legal labor relationship is regulated by the legal documents that establish
the institutional framework of the employer and employee
coordinates as the subject of law, as well as by legal acts
that are based on the free will of parties to conclude con-

tracts (collective agreements and individual employment contracts).

The individual employment contract is further distinguished as important within the sources of the legal work relationship. It maintains the role of main designer of this legal relationship. General rules governing the legal relationship of employment are impersonal and insufficient to determine the specific rights and obligations of the parties.

They are key elements that can only be established by free will of the parties, reflected by the conclusion of an individual contract of employment. By its consensual nature, concluding an individual employment contract is a legal expression of freedom of labor principle.

Parties of an individual employment contract are separated. Only the conclusion of this legal act creates the legal framework necessary to achieve their goals and interests, essentially divergent. The individual employment contract is the legal instrument by which they will cross their legal will to exercise rights and to meet obligations in order to obtain benefits. The legal rights and obligations of the legal relationship parties, stipulated by legislation or by regulations and statutes, are applicable only to an established legal relationship. This relationship is concrete, established between the employee and employer only as effect of the individual employment contract. Elements such as the type of work, salary, duration of employment relationship can be established only by contract, which becomes the law of the parties. Rights and obligations of employer and employee are respected only by executing the individual employment contract.

The individual employment contract is presented as a legal instrument which reflects the rights and obligations of two legal parties, employer and employee.It is intended to stimulate the parties in the continuous achievement of the terms established. Experience confirms that if the contracting parties have unequivocal knowledge of the mutual rights and obligations, they are likely to avoid subsequent complaints or disputes, with all the range of effects that they produce [7].

The individual employment contract remains the main source of individual legal labor relations[8]. It is a result of the fact that labor market dynamics should be reflected in the new meanings of rights and obligations of the parties, which can not be covered by legal acts, with their general and impersonal character. The purpose of the legal work relationship is a special one, connected to the personality of human beings, and, as people are different, we need individual legal acts which materialize working conditions in which each of the employees provides work.

II.   Characteristics of the individual employment contract

Characteristics of the individual employment contract are those features that define and customize it in relation to other civil or commercial contracts also involving the provision of work.

The International Labour Organisation has given priority to the individual employment contract concluded for an indefinite period and full-time. It is the legal instrument that re-

---

[7] S. Ghimpu, G. Mohanu, Condiţiile încheierii contractului individual de muncă, Editura ştiinţifică şi enciclopedică, Bucureşti, 1988, p. 133-134

[8] See, in this regard, I.T. Ştefănescu, Tratat de dreptul muncii, Wolters Kluwer Publishing House, Bucureşti, 2007, p. 191; Al. Ţiclea, Tratat de dreptul muncii, Rosetti Publishing House, Bucureşti, 2006, p. 303; Al. Athanasiu, L. Dima, Dreptul muncii, ALL Beck Publishing House, Bucureşti, 2005, p. 24

sponds best to the principle of protecting the employee in the relationship of subordination created in the contract. The ILO vision on the duration of the work is found for the first time in the Recommendation 166/1982. Member States were invited to establish adequate safeguards against the use of fixed-term employment contracts. Given this recommendation, but also the fact that the overwhelming majority of ILO member States circumscribe their legislation to this principle, the rule on employment contracts implies employment contracts of indefinite duration. In the context of globalization and considering the pressure of unprecedented economic development, materialized in increased competition between operators, flexible labor relations appear to be a necessity. These labour relations imply the use of fixed-term employment contracts, part-time temporary employment agencies or labor at home. Although aware of all these transformations, the ILO continued to address in its work, mostly, the issue of individual employment contract of indefinite duration[9].

At the ILO Conference in 1998 it was tried for the first time to regulate the employment relationship of those who perform an activity or provide a service under a civil or commercial contract. What was only obtained was keeping this problem in the attention of the organization.

Thus, in 2003, the ILO recommended Member States to adopt policies that prohibit the practice of concealing the employment relationship, practices that have as effect the absence or reduction of social protection for workers, which is only provided by employment law.

---

[9] For details of I.L.O. action, see A. Popescu, Drept internațional al muncii, C.H Beck Publishing House, București, 2006, p. 227-234

Within the ILO Conference in 2006 Recommendation 198 was adopted, regarding work relationships. This Recommendation requires Member States to formulate and implement, after consultation with social partners, special national policies. They would allow the determination of the specific employment relationship, would formulate criteria to distinguish between employees and self-employed workers. Measures to combat disguised employment relationships and to adopt rules applicable to all forms of contractual arrangements would be thus established[10].

The Recommendation states that it is necessary to adopt a national policy to protect workers within employment relationships.This statement starts from the consideration that, in some cases, difficulties in establishing an employment relationship occur, either because rights and obligations of the parties are not clearly defined, or because there are attempts to disguise the employment relationship, or even because the law, its interpretation or application is insufficient or limited, all these making workers vulnerable. In the second part, the Recommendation 198/2006 of ILO states the determination of the existence of an employment relationship by conditions and by specific indicators[11].

---

[10] A. Popescu, Drept internaţional al muncii, C.H. Beck Publishing House, Bucureşti, 2006, p. 231-232
[11] A. Popescu, Drept internaţional al muncii, C.H. Beck Publishing House, Bucureşti, 2006, p. 233

Title II
Conclusion Of The Individual Work Contract

Chapter 1
Conditions Necessary For The Valid Conclusion of The Individual Work Contract

The conditions of validity represent a set of requirements that ensure the employment contract the full production of legal effects. In this respect, the legal conditions to be fulfilled for the valid conclusion of the individual labor contract are mostly common to all contracts of different branches of law, while others are specific only to labor law.

The common conditions are the ability, the subject, the consent and the cause. The specific conditions are the existence of the job, professional training, work experience and experience in the field, passing an examination, the contest, the approval, the licensing, the certificate and the physical and mental preparation of the person who requires employment.

I.   The contracting parties' ability

The parties' ability to conclude the employment contract is an essential condition for the validity of this legal act. The individual and the legal capacity are considered   either in terms of use, that is,   the general and abstract ability of a person to have rights and obligations, or in terms of capacity for exercise.

The latter refers to the possibility of exercising rights and obligations by committing legal acts[12]. Moreover, the capacity should be analyzed in terms of both contracting parties, tak-

---

[12] Gh. Beleiu, Drept civil român. Introducere în dreptul civil. Subiectele dreptului civil, 7th ed., revised and enlarged by Marian Nicolae and Petrică Trușcă, Universul Juridic Publishing House, București, 2001, p. 32

Guide for Romanian and German Labour Law
Basics of the Employment Relationship

ing into account the rights and obligations they have by concluding the individual employment contract.

I.1. The legal capacity of the person to be employed

The legal solution to this problem is found primarily in the Civil code. According to art. 42[13], the minor may conclude legal documents on labor, sports, artistic pursuits or on his profession, with the consent of parents or of a guardian, and with the provisions of special laws, if applicable. The minor exercises his rights and thus performs all the obligations arising from these acts and can use the received income.

At the same time, the *intuitu personae* character of the individual employment contract results in the indissoluble link between the capacity utilization and the exercise capacity of the person to become employed. This is a result of work being by definition personal, not to be accomplished by another person. Considering these aspects, the doctrine stated that in the legal relationship of employment, the legal capacity of the person to be employed can be considered unique[14].

The legal capacity to conclude employment contracts is subject to the biophysical capacity to work[15]. In this regard, the Labour Code establishes in Art. 13 that the individual becomes able to work at the age of 16.

---

[13] Gh. Beleiu, Drept civil român. Introducere în dreptul civil. Subiectele dreptului civil, 7th ed., revised and enlarged by Marian Nicolae and Petrică Trușcă, Universul Juridic Publishing House, București, 2001, p. 32

[14] S. Ghimpu Gh Mohanu, Condițiile încheierii contractului individual de muncă, Editura științifică și enciclopedică, București, 1988, p. 20; C. Tufan, Reglementări juridice privind încheierea contractului individual de muncă, in „Raporturi de muncă" no. 8/1997, p. 55; S. Ghimpu, Al. Țiclea, Dreptul muncii, 2 nd ed., All Beck Publishing House, București, 2002, p. 165

[15] N. Voiculescu, Dreptul muncii – Reglementări interne și comunitare, Rosetti Publishing House, București, 2003, p. 17-18

The Labour Code, in conjunction with the Constitutional and with the Civil Code expressly provides that an individual may conclude an employment contract as an employee working at the age of 15, if certain conditions are met. Firstly, there is the consent of parents or of legal representatives. Secondly, the contract is concluded for activities appropriate to the physical development, to the skills and knowledge of the minor person. Finally, by the work performed, the minor's health, development and professional training are not endangered.

To sum up, between the age of 15 and 16 the individual has a limited capacity to conclude an individual employment contract as an employee. Parental consent for the minor's employment must be prior or concomitant to the conclusion of the individual employment contract. This consent must be special, that is, it must target a particular contract and it must also be express, that is, have a clear, precise form[16].

In the national labor law, the capacity of the person to be employed is subject to the minimum age and, in some cases, to certain incompatibilities established by law, but there is no upper age limit generally applicable.

a)   Incompatibilities

Incompatibilities are those limitations or restrictions of legal capacity, expressly and strictly regulated by law, in order to protect the person and defense general interests of society. Incompatibilities are not presumed, can not be deduced by

---

[16] I.T. Stefănescu, Tratat de dreptul muncii, Wolters Kluwer Publishing House, Bucureşti, 2007, p. 300; Al. Athanasiu, C. A. Moarcăş, Muncitorul şi legea, Oscar Print Publishing House, Bucureşti, 1999, p. 46-47, Al. Athanasiu, L. Dima, Dreptul muncii, All Beck Publishing House, Bucureşti, 2005, p. 32-37; Al. Ţiclea, A. Popescu, M. Ţichindelean, C. Tufan, O. Ţinca, Dreptul muncii, Rosetti Publishing House, Bucureşti, 2004, p. 338 et seq.

Guide for Romanian and German Labour Law
Basics of the Employment Relationship

analogy and can not be extended. This is expressly and strictly regulated by law, operating only in the conditions and time periods provided in its content[17]. If inconsistencies are applied other than in limited circumstances prescribed by law, this would be a violation of the constitutional principle of freedom of labor[18].

The Labor Code does not regulate situations of incompatibility on concluding employment contracts. Prohibitions are emphasized by other acts belonging to the labor legislation and to the administrative, commercial or criminal legislation.

Given the above mentioned, it can be concluded that the effect of a situation of incompatibility of a person seeking employment is materialized in the legal impossibility to validly conclude a certain individual employment contract as an employee. Violation of these prohibitions leads to absolute nullity of the individual employment contract and, therefore, to the termination of contract, on avoidance, amicably or judicially.

b)   Concurrent positions

Concurrent positions refer to that situation in which the same individual is employed simultaneously based on two or more individual employment contracts. The Labor Code governing concurrent positions in art. 35 covers only work under individual employment contracts.

In accordance with art. 35 of Labor Code the rule in labor relations is the admissibility of concurrent positions, based on individual employment contracts. The employee benefits

---

[17] Al. Ţiclea, Tratat de dreptul muncii, Rosetti Publishing House, Bucureşti, 2006, p. 48-49
[18] See Constitutional Court Decision on the constitutionality of some provisions of Law no. 51/1995 regarding the organization and exercise of the profession of attorney, re-published in Official Gazette of Romania, no. 98, February 7, 2011

from the salary corresponding to each of them. Concurrent positions are allowed for all employees, regardless of the nature or quality of employers[19], but with some exceptions.

According to art. 35 para. 2 of the Labor Code, however, situations in which there are legal incompatibilities for concurrent positions are exceptions to the rule. Employees who have more positions have the right to choose their main function and have the obligation to declare it to each employer, according to tax laws. The doctrine stated that the employee cannot choose discretionary their main position. The employer's agreement is necessary[20], as the latter ensures the employee certain rights, other than salary. Therefore, this employer applies the tax deductions on salary tax calculation.

The employee having more positions based on individual contracts of employment concluded with different employers may change the main position from one employer to another during the execution of these contracts, under the law.

The Labour Code makes no distinction between the duties of the employer where the main position is held and the one where the position is concurrent, both having the obligation to provide the employee all employment rights, thus an equal treatment between employers is ensured, on the one hand, and also between employees with main positions and those with concurrent positions on the other hand.

II.2. Legal capacity of the employer

The employer is the part of the individual labor contract that benefits from the work performed by an employee under his

---

[19] See in this respect, Al. Ţiclea, Tratat de dreptul muncii, Rosetti Publishing House București, 2006, p. 121
[20] Al. Ţiclea, Tratat de dreptul muncii, Rosetti Publishing House, București, 2006, p. 149

authority, who must ensure the conditions necessary for employees to work in safety, and to remunerate the work done by them. The employer, regardless of the legal form of organization and its specificity, must have legal capacity in order to be part of an individual contract. The Labour Code, art. 14 para. 1 specifies that the employer may be a legal entity or natural person, which means that the problem of employer capacity is seen differently, depending on the category they fall into. It should be noted, before analyzing the legal capacity of a legal person employer and that of an individual employer, that having a legal entity employer is the common situation in labor relations.

a) The legal entity employer

In accordance with art. 14 para. 2 of the Labor Code the legal person may conclude an individual contract of employment as an employer once they acquire their legal personality.

The legal person has, as an individual, one capacity of utilization and one of exercise. According to art. 206 para. 1 of the Romanian Civil Code, the legal person may have any civil rights and obligations, except those which by their nature or by law, are only found in the individual. According to para. 2 of the same article, non-profit legal entities may have only those rights and obligations necessary for the purpose established by law, articles of incorporation or statute. Legal acts concluded in breach of these statutory provisions are absolutely void. From the perspective of labor law, the principle of capacity of usage specialty of the non-profit legal person is supposed to include only people whose skills and training can ensure reaching the purpose for which they were established.

The exercise capacity of the legal entity is the ability of the collective subject to exercise rights and fulfill obligations by legal acts concluded by its management bodies, after their creation. According to art. 209 of the Civil Code, the legal entity exercises rights and fulfils its obligations through its management bodies. The quality of management bodies is possessed by natural or legal persons. These persons are, by law, by articles of incorporation or status, entitled to act in relation to third parties, individually or collectively and on behalf of the legal person. Relationships between the legal entity and those who make up its management bodies are analogous to the mandate rules, unless otherwise provided by law, articles of incorporation or statute (Art. 209 para. 3 of the Civil Code).

The analysis shows that for all legal persons, the individual employment contracts are concluded on their behalf by the head unit, or by the collective management body. If the employment contract was concluded by a person who is not a management body of the legal person, or by a person who was given such a mandate, but who exceeded his powers, the contract is relatively null and void. Nullity may be covered by countersigning the individual employment contract by the person entitled to such tasks.

The legal person may delegate power to conclude individual contracts of employment to its units without legal personality (branches, agencies, offices). This delegation must be explicit and specific. Thus, art. 2 para. 3 of Government Decision no. 500/2011 on the general registry of employees[21] states that employers who delegated their own entities without legal personality the authority to hire by concluding individual contracts of employment, may delegate them the power of setting the registry.

b) The individual employer

The Labour Code, when mentioning the employer, considers not only the legal entity but also the individual, stating that this individual, in order to conclude individual work contracts, must have full legal capacity (Art. 14 para. 3 Labour Code). Therefore, to detail the legal provisions mentioned, it is necessary to interpret them in relation to the civil code relating to the individual.

According to art. 37 of this law, the exercise capacity is the ability of the person to conclude civil legal acts. The analysis of legal text shows that the legislature considered, when drafting the Labour Code, the full legal capacity of the individual. As the full legal capacity is acquired at the age of 18, it means that, before reaching this age, children cannot act as employers, except when, in special cases, they acquire full legal capacity before the age of 18 (married child aged 16 to 18 years, according to art. 39 of the Civil Code).

I.3. Limitations of the legal capacity of individuals to individual employment contracts as an employer

Exceptionally, the law can make use of the capacity limitations of the individual. Regarding labor relations, what is of great interest is the limitation of use of the individual. This is

---

[21] Published in the Official Gazette of Romania, Part I, no. 372, May 27, 2011, amended by Government Decision no. 1105/2011, published in Official Gazette of Romania, Part I, no. 798, November 10, 2011

Guide for Romanian and German Labour Law
Basics of the Employment Relationship

contained in art. 28 para. 4 of the Government Emergency Ordinance no. 44/2008[22] on economic activities performed by authorized individuals, sole proprietorships and family businesses.

According to the legal provision mentioned, the family business may not employ a third party with a work contract. This legal prohibition applies only to the conclusion of individual labor contracts aimed at activities authorized. There is no limitation to the use of the natural capacity of the individual employer to conclude employment contracts for domestic workers, at his home, unrelated to the activities for which authorization was obtained under this law.

The analyzed prohibition, representing a capacity limitation of the individual, must be interpreted strictly, which means that individuals who are not traders, are not affected by this regulatory provision.

In conclusion, the person hiring under an individual contract of employment, is called an employer, in accordance with the Labor Code. Both a legal and an individual person may be an employer. The synonym that is used, both in law and in literature is that of patron. In this respect the definition of a patron given by art. 1 letter v) of Law no. 62/2011 of social dialogue[23] should be mentioned. According to that definition, the patron is the legal registered owner, an individual person authorized by law or the person exercising a craft or a profession independently, managing and using capital for profit under competition and who undertakes employment.

---

[22] Published in Official Gazette of Romania, Part I, no. 328, April 25, 2008, amended later
[23] Law no. 62/2011 of social dialogue, republished in Official Gazette of Romania, no. 625, August 31, 2012

II. Consent of the parties on concluding the individual labor contract

For an individual contract to be concluded legally it is necessary that both parties will be expressed validly, unambiguously and in full knowledge. Agreement of the two parties must be made under the law. According to art. 16 para. 1 of the Labour Code 'the individual labor contract is concluded with the parties consent, in writing, in Romanian'.

In accordance with Directive 91/533/EEC[24], the Labour Code governs the employer's obligation to inform the employee prior to termination or modification of the individual work contract[25], on the essential elements of the individual employment contract. This information is in fact a genuine offer to contract, designed to lead to the formation of the future employed person's consent to conclude the employment contract.

The employer's offer must meet all conditions of consent, namely:

- to be a manifestation of real, serious, conscious will, with intent to legally employ;

- to be firm, that is, to contain an undoubted commitment;

- to be unequivocal, showing that it is an offer, without having a different meaning;

- to be precise and complete, that is, to contain all the elements, so that, by accepting it, it would lead to the concluding of the contract.

---

[24] Council Directive 91/533/EEC of 14 October 1991 on an employer's obligation to inform employees of the conditions applicable to the contract or employment relationship, published in Official Journal of the European Union, Series L 288, October 10, 1991
[25] See, for common law, V. Patulea, Obligația de informare în formarea contractelor, in „Revista de drept comercial" no. 6/1998, p. 75 et seq.

The employee also has the obligation to inform the employer, before concluding the individual labor contract, regarding his personal information, although this is not expressly provided by the Labor Code[26].

The consent is the essential background and general condition of the civil act that consists of the externally manifested determination to conclude a legal act[27]. In terms of terminology, it is worth noting that the term "consent" means, in the individual employment contract, the agreement of the two parties to conclude it. The individual employment contract is considered valid if concluded at the time of the agreement between the employer and the one who will require employment, even if filing documents is made after this time.

Agreement of the parties to conclude the individual labor contract must be in accordance with civil law. Thus, in order to be valid, the consent of both the employer and the one seeking employment must come from someone with discernment. It must also be expressed with the intention to produce legal effects and be externalized and unaltered by any vice of consent (mistake, fraud, violence).

a. Consent must be from a person with legal judgment, a person who has the power to judge and discern legal effects that occur under his manifestation of will. This condition of validity of consent arises from the conscious character of the legal act.

The individual with full legal capacity shall be presumed to have legal judgment necessary to perform legal acts. The

---

[26] See I.T Ştefănescu, Tratat de dreptul muncii, Wolters Kluwer Publishing House, Bucureşti, 2007, p. 213

[27] Gh. Beleiu, Drept civil român. Introducere în dreptul civil. Subiectele dreptului civil, 7th ed., revised and enlarged by Marian Nicolae and Petrică Truşcă, Legal Publishing House, Bucureşti, 2001, p.146; G. Boroi, Drept civil. Partea generală. Persoanele, All Beck Publishing House, Bucureşti, 2001, p. 160-172

person lacking the legal capacity (minors under 14 years and individuals placed under judicial prohibition) is presumed to have no discernment, due to young age or mental health.

Minors between 14 and 18 years has a developing discernment. In labor law, however, the minor aged 16 years is presumed to have the necessary legal judgment necessary for concluding individual employment contracts as an employee.

For the legal body there are no legal judgement issues, because the legal representative is always a person with full legal capacity.

b. Consent must be serious, expressed freely and knowingly, with intent to produce legal effects. This condition stems from the essence of the legal act, which is a manifestation of the will made with the intention to produce legal effects, ie to create, modify or extinguish a specific legal relationship, namely a legal work relationship.

c. The consent must be externalized, a condition which results from its definition. The decision to conclude the employment contract must not remain only at the mental level, but must be expressed. Also, lack of consent expression, that is, silence, is not an agreement on the termination of employment contract under the conditions proposed by the negotiating partner.

Externalization of the consent to conclude an individual contract is the written form, as a condition of validity of the individual employment contract, according to art. 16 para. 1 of the Labor Code.

d. The consent shall not be affected by any vice of consent, as an expression of freedom of the legal act, of its conscious conclusion. In accordance with art. 1206 of the Civil Code vics of consent are considered the error, fraud, deceit and injury.

A feature of vices of consent is the fact that the manifestation of will exists, but it is altered either in its intellectual content, such as the case of deception and error, or in its free character, such as the case of violence and injury[28].

III.   The subject and cause of the individual labor contract

Another mandatory general condition of conclusion of the individual labor contract is the subject of the contract. According to art. 1225 para. 1 of the Civil Code, the subject of the contract is the legal operation agreed by the parties as revealed by assembled contractual rights and obligations. According to art. 1226 of the Civil Code, the subject of the obligation is the performance that the debtor undertakes. Although the purpose and content of the juridical act are closely related, the actions or omissions to which parties are entitled should not be confused with the rights and obligations that the legal act rises and that form the content or effects of the civil act.

For validity of the contract it is necessary that the subject be legitimate and determined or at least ascertainable and lawful. The Labor Code, art. 15, with a mandatory provision, prohibits, under penalty of nullity, concluding an individual labor contract for the provision of illicit or immoral activities.

The individual employment contract is a mutually binding contract, for the mutual benefit of the parties, meaning work performed by the employee and his salary by the employer. These two elements are inseparable.

---

[28] See, in this respect, Gh. Beleiu, Drept civil român. Introducere în dreptul civil. Subiectele dreptului civil, 7th ed., revised and enlarged by Marian Nicolae and Petrică Truşcă, Universul Juridic Publishing House, Bucureşti, 2001, p. 158

The two services are in a direct and indissoluble connection, and if an individual employment contract would not include one of these two elements, it would be null[29]. Work performed by the employee, as the object of the individual employment contract, must be executed under legitimate conditions, without affecting the morality or public order. An individual employment contract that would have as a subject the provision of an activity prohibited by the labor law is null and void and can not produce any legal effect.

In the individual contract of employment, the employee is obliged to provide any service connected with the occupation for which he was employed. Of course, the employer may require his employee to perform only that work for which he was bound by the contract, work that is in accordance with his skills, even if he may be trained for other activities as well.

Labor remuneration by the employer is the second essential element of the individual labor contract subject, representing money paid for work provided under the individual employment contract. Salary must be paid to the employee, even if not expressly mentioned in the contract, as far as his work was provided and it is clear that the intention was to conclude an individual contract.

By regulating the correlation between work performed by the employee and salary paid by the employer the principle of equivalence of benefits in reciprocal obligations contracts is respected.

The subject matter is a prerequisite to concluding any contract, and, therefore, to concluding an individual labor con-

---

[31] Al. Athahasiu, L. Dima, Dreptul muncii, All Beck Publishing House, Bucureşti, 2005, p. 39; Al. Ţiclea, Tratat de dreptul muncii, Rosetti Publishing House, Bucureşti, 2006, p. 73

tract. According to art. 1235 in the Civil Code, the subject matter is the reason that determines each party to conclude the contract. With the consent the the subject matter forms the legal will. The subject matter is the element that answers the question why the contract was concluded. As an essential condition of the contract, the subject matter is not confused with consent or with the object of such an act, which means that it is an independent element. The subject matter mustexist, be lawful and moral, according to art. 1236 in the Civil Code.

The Labor Code expressly refers to the individual labor contract in art. 15. It states that it is forbidden, under pain of nullity, to conclude an individual labor contract for the provision of work or illicit or immoral activities. In case of violations of these rules the penalty involved is the absolute nullity of the individual employment contract, revocation which will take effect only for the future.

In the case of the individual employment contract the cause lies in the aim sought by each party by signing this legal document, namely: financial resources necessary for living, in terms of the employee and the employee work performance, in terms of the employer.

IV.   The form of the individual employment contract

The form of the individual labor contract means that condition of the legal act that consists of the means to externalize the manifestation of the parties' will with the intention to create, modify or extinguish a legal work relationship.

The form of the individual employment contract is the written form, required for stating a written contract, according to art. 1241 of the Civil Code . According to art. 16 para. 1 of the Labor Code, the written form of the individual employment contract is required for its valid conclusion. Lack of the written form affects the validity of the individual employment contract itself.

Chapter 2
Specific Conditions Necessary For The Valid Conclusion Of The Individual Labor Contract

As stated earlier, for the conclusion of a legal and valid employment contract a   number of conditions must be met. Some of these are common to the valid conclusion of any contract (capacity, object, consent and case), while others are specific to the individual employment contract. In this respect we should mention conditions such as the existence of the job, training, work experience, specialized skills and professional knowledge check, medical examination, conditions for certain categories of employees.

I.   The medical examination

In order to be party of a legal work relationship, in which the individual is obliged to carry out certain activities on behalf of the employer, involves not only the legal capacity, but also the ability to work in a biological sense. That implies the physical and mental ability of the one providing work.

ividuals may be employed only under a medical certificate confirming that their health allows them to perform the work they are entrusted (Article 27 para. 1 Labour Code). Furthermore, Law no. 319/2006[30]   on health and safety at work, states the obligation of the employer to employ only people who, after the medical examination and verification of psy-

---

[30] Published in Official Gazette of Romania, Part I, no. 646, July 26, 2006

chosocial skills, will correspond to the task to be fulfilled. By Government Decision no. 355/2007[31] on workers' health surveillance, the procedure for medical examination of workers, both in employment and during the execution of the individual employment contract was regulated. Article 9 para. 1 of the Decision defines the ability to work, stating that it represents the medical capacity of a worker to perform an activity in the profession / function for which the medical examination is required.

The Labor Code provides in art. 27 para. 2 that the conclusion of an employment contract without medical examination is sanctioned by absolute nullity of the contract. Transposing EU rules on equal treatment and on the prohibition of discrimination, the Labour Code expressly prohibits the employment request of pregnancy tests (Art. 27 para. 5). Subsequently to employment, pregnant women benefit from special protection measures on maternal risk[32].

As an additional measure to protect the health of workers, the Labor Code provides in art. 28 the compulsoriness of medical examination during the execution or modification of the individual labor contract in the following cases:

- for the resumption of work after a break of more than 6 months for jobs with professional exposure to harmful factors, and in other cases, of a one year break;

- for secondment or transfer to another job or other activity;

- at the beginning of activity for temporary employment contract employees;

---

[31] Published in Official Gazette of Romania, Part I, no. 322, May 17, 2007
[32] Government Emergency Ordinance no. 96/2003 on maternity protection at work, published in Official Gazette of Romania, Part I, no. 750, October 27, 2003, approved with amendments by Law no. 25/2004, amended by Government Emergency Ordinance no. 158/2005 on leave and health insurance allowances, published in Official Gazette of Romania, Part I, no. 1074, November 29, 2005

-for apprentices, interns, students and pupils, if they are to be trained in trades and professions, as well as in the situation of a job change during the training;

- periodically, for those who work under conditions of exposure to occupational harmful factors, according to Ministry of Health regulations;

- periodically, for those working in units with no risk factors, through medical exams differentiated by age, sex and health status, as determined by regulations in collective agreements.

Analyzing all legal provisions in the field of medical examination of the person seeking employment, both before the conclusion of the individual labor contract and during its execution, we find that the legislature, giving expression to the principle of protection of the person who performs the work, imposed a series of obligations to the employer, establishing severe penalties for violations.

II. Checking personal skills and professional training of individuals applying for employment

The Labor Code governs the condition of personal and professional skills verification of the person seeking employment, before the conclusion of the individual labor contract (art. 29). This condition imposed by law for the valid conclusion of a contract is specific to labor law.

Ways to achieve this check are not expressly established by the framework law in labor relations. This only makes reference to regulations of the collective agreement applicable, to personal status and to the internal rules of each employer. As in other cases, the Labour Code states only the directions to be followed, leaving the social sides of the labor market the possibility to regulate the concrete conditions under which professional and personal skills of those seeking employment will be checked. Therefore, any means deemed by the employer or by the social partners suitable for the work performed may be established for checking. These means are: competition, the exam, the interview and the practical test.

Checking the professional and personal skills of the person seeking employment can be made by any of the methods listed, except for public sector and budgetary units employees, where employment is made only through competition or examination (Article 30 para. 1 Labour Code). Regarding this regulatory provision, which allows verification of professional skills in the public institutions and other budgetary units by examination, it is to be mentioned that it triggered criticism from different union representatives who considered inserting this provision in the Labour Code an open door to abuse and corruption in the public system.

However, the fear of union representatives had no legal support. Employment in the public sector of contractual staff is established by law. The provision of the Labor Code would not have been necessary, as long as there is a special law governing employment by examination or contest of the vacant positions in public institutions. It is true that certain conditions must be met for entry to contest or examination, but the interest protected by the legal norm is a public one and the additional requirements imposed by law are justified, in relation to the ones in the private sector.

Accordingly, for the institutions, public authorities and other budgetary units the professional check through competition or exam remains mandatory, as it is the only way to verify the

professional and personal skills of the person seeking employment. For the personnel in certain categories of budgetary units, conditions of employment are provided by special
laws. When staffing is necessary, job vacancies are open for
competition, are made public and communicated to employment agencies, detailing the specific conditions of organization and participation in the contest. If in the contest
for filling a vacancy several candidates have not been registered, verifying the only candidate's professional and personal skills is done by examination[33].

For autonomous divisions, for companies and other legal persons, other than the budgetary ones, employment is made by
the conditions established in the articles of association, in internal regulations or in the applicable collective labor contract, if the law does not provide otherwise.

By regulating the means of verifying the professional and
personal skills of the person applying for employment, the organizational prerogative of the employer is reinforced, as a
right recognized as legal. Having the right to determine the
organization and functioning of the unit, as an exclusive
right, the employer is directly given the recruitment right[34].

III. Approval, work permit and commitment

There are situations when, for concluding an individual work
contract covering performance of a specific activity, it is
necessary to have a prior approval, authorization or certifi-

---

[33] See, in this regard, the Government Decision no. 281/1993 on the remuneration of staff in budgetary units, published in Official Gazette of Romania, Part I, no. 135, June 25, 1993, with subsequent amendments
[34] M. Volonciu, Comment (to art. 29) in Al. Athanasiu, M. Volonciu, L. Dima, O. Cazan Codul muncii, Comentariu pe articole, vol. I art. 1-107, C.H. Beck Publishing House, Bucureşti, 2007

cate issued by institutions authorized to do so by various regulatory provisions.

Thus, the police approval is necessary for the employment of security guards to be armed with weapons, for private security personnel[35], for gaming venue staff. Police approval is binding; failure to achieve the conditions for obtaining it lead to nullity of the individual labor contract that is absolute, but remediable.

Compulsory withdrawal shall have the effect of termination of the individual employment contract.

The withdrawal of the police approval leads to termination of the individual labor contract.

This withdrawal can be made only if a legal provision expressly provides it, the interest protected by law being in the case a public one[36].

One category of approval before the conclusion of the individual labor contract is given by the other managers, if management is entrusted to several people or by the manager when there are subordinated people employed. In this case, however, an approval is optional; the hiring party is not bound to consider it.

If an approval is necessary for obtaining a job, in other cases an authorization/professional certification is required for concluding an individual employment contract. Thus, for the quality of shot firer it is necessary to obtain the authorization of the territorial labor inspectorate[37]. For the securities authorized agent, the authorization of the National Securities

---

[35] Law no. 333/2003 on the protection of objectives, goods, values and personal protection, republished in Official Gazette of Romania, no. 189, March 18, 2014
[36] Al. Țiclea, Tratat de dreptul muncii, Rosetti Publishing House, București, 2006, p. 80
[37] Article 27 of Law no. 126/1995 on the regime of explosive materials, republished in Official Gazette of Romania, no. 177, March 12, 2014, amended and supplemented

Commission[38] is required. For the professional foster the professional certification of Child Protection Commission is to be obtained. For the tour guide the certification of the Ministry of Resort is necessary. To obtain these certifications it is mandatory that the person requesting one of them meets certain conditions evaluated by competent authorities.

Thus, for the certificate of a professional foster[39] care particular conditions are required and maintained during the execution of the individual employment contract, under penalty of suspension or termination of contract.

The conditions relate to the moral profile of the applicant, to their state of health and professional training. The enactment states that the applicant must be secure for the proper performance of the duties of a parent in relation to raising and educating children. It also requires that the foster certifies by medical examination the absence of any communicable chronic diseases. As professional training on application, the applicant must have at least a secondary education, during evaluation the graduation of the training course being also required.

Authorization/certification must be considered, as the approval prior to conclusion of the individual labor contract, through the effects produced by the failure to meet the mandatory requirement imposed by law. As in the case of the approval, the existence of no authorization/certification leads to nullity of the individual employment contract, nullity that is absolute, but remediable. It should be also noted that

---

[38] Article 13 of Regulation no. 3/1996 on the authorization and exercise of securities brokerage, approved by Order no. 15/1996 of the National Securities Commission, published in Official Gazette of Romania, Part I, no. 176, August 5, 1996
[39] See, in this regard, the Government Decision no. 679/2003 on conditions for obtaining a certificate of professional maternal assistant, certification procedures and professional caregiver status, published in Official Gazette of Romania, Part I, no. 443, June 23, 2003

the prior approval and authorization/certification are compulsory for all employers, since these legal rules are binding. Regulations that condition the validity of an employment contract on the existence of an approval, of an authorization or of a certificate, prior or concomitant with termination of contract, are mandatory and binding for all employers. Failure to comply with these regulations is punished with individual employment contract invalidity and, therefore, the contract will be terminated as from the date of the finding of invalidity, either amicably or judicially.

Withdrawal of approval, authorization or certification during the execution of the individual employment contract or expiry of the time limit for which they were issued, result in termination of the individual labor contract according to art. 56 letter h) of the Labor Code. This termination occurs regardless of the culpable attitude of the employee.

 Refusal to issue the approval or authorization and their withdrawal by the authorities empowered to grant them may be appealed to the administrative courts.

Regarding the work permit, employment of foreigners is done according to art. 2 letters c) and d) of the Labor Code, of the Government Emergency Ordinance no. 194/2002 on the regime of foreigners in Romania[40] and of the Government Emergency Ordinance no. 56/2007 on the employment and deployment of foreigners in Romania[41]. Foreigners are people who do not have Romanian citizenship or nationality of another Member State of the European Union or of the European Economic Area.

---

[40] Republished in Official Gazette of Romania, Part I, no. 421, June 5, 2008
[41] Published in Official Gazette of Romania, Part I, no. 424, June, 26, 2007

The work permit is an official document issued under the law that entitles the holder to be employed or seconded to Romania by one employer.

Foreigners can be employed in Romania to employers who operate legally, with the following cumulative conditions:

a) vacancies cannot be filled by Romanian citizens, or by citizens of other European Union Member States, of the states that signed the Agreement on the European Economic Area, and by any permanent residents in Romania;

b) they must comply with specific training, work experience and approval conditions required by the employer under the legislation in force;

c) prove that they are medically able to carry out their activity and have no criminal record to be incompatible with the work they do in Romania;

d) fall in annual quota approved by Government Decision;

e) employers have paid to date obligations to the state budget.

The provisions of paragraph a) shall not apply to foreigners who act as administrators in a company with foreign participation, where only one person is appointed to this position, if the foreigner is working as a professional athlete, given the existence of evidence that similar activity was conducted in another country, for work permit applicants, for cross-border workers and for foreigners holding a residence permit for study purposes.

The following categories of individuals may be employed or, if necessary, can provide work to individuals or legal entities in Romania without a work permit:

a) foreigners holding permanent residence rights in Romania;

b) foreigners whose access to the labor market in Romania is regulated by agreements, conventions or bilateral agreements concluded by Romania with other states, if this option is set by the text of the agreement or of the convention;

c) foreigners who were granted a form of protection in Romania;

d) foreigners with teaching or scientific activities, or other specific categories of temporary work activities in specialized institutions accredited in Romania, based on bilateral agreements, or as a holder of a right of residence to conduct scientific research and high staff qualified by order of the Minister of Education, Research and Youth, and foreigners performing artistic activities in cultural institutions in Romania by order of the Minister of Culture;

e) foreigners who are to carry out temporary activities in Romania requested by ministries or other government bodies or local or autonomous authorities;

f) foreigners who are appointed heads of branches, representative offices and branches in Romania of a company that is based abroad, in accordance with provisions of the Romanian law;

g) foreign family members of Romanian citizens;

h) foreign employees of legal entities established in a Member State of the European Union or in one of the signatory states of the Agreement on the European Economic Area, posted in Romania, on presentation of residence in that State.

Application for the work permit shall be settled by the Romanian Immigration Office within 30 days from the date of filing. In some cases, for considering that all the conditions for obtaining the work permit were met, additional checks are required and the request may be extended by 15 days.

The work permit is issued for a period of one year, excepting the case of seasonal workers.

The work permit is automatically extended for additional periods of up to one year in the situation of employment with the same employer, on the individual labor contract concluded for an indefinite period, by extending the right of residence for work. It is attested by a residence permit issued for this purpose.

In the case of individual contracts of employment concluded for a limited period of time, work authorization is extended for the period requested and cannot be longer than one year and longer than the validity of the contract. For extension of authorization beyond the original validity period of the contract the written agreement of the parties is required, regarding the extension of the contract concluded under the Labor Code, as amended and supplemented.

Employing foreigners without a work permit by a natural or legal person in Romania is a contravention and is punishable by fine.

Romanian labor laws and social security laws apply to foreigners legally employed in Romania on the basis of work permits, with the same rights as Romanian employees and the same general obligations that arise from the individual employment contracts, any discrimination of these employees against Romanian workers or community being prohibited.

Written commitment of state and service secrecy

Observance of professional secrecy is a general obligation of employees provided by art. Article 39 para 2 letter f) of the Labor Code, but for a special category of employees that requirement must be embodied in a document.

By this document the person to be employed in a job that requires access to classified information should present the employer a written commitment of secrecy. In the absence of a written commitment the employment contract will be impossible to be concluded, even if the other conditions required by law for the valid conclusion of the legal act in question are met. The commitment of state and service secrecy can be assumed both when concluding the individual employment contract and during its execution, when it implies moving to a new job is which involves access to classified information, classified according to Law no.182 / 2002[42].

IV.   Probation

To verify employee skills, the individual employment contract may establish a probationary period not exceeding 90 calendar days for executive positions and a maximum of 120 calendar days for management positions (Article 32 Labour Code). For unskilled workers probation is exceptional in nature and may not exceed 5 days.

For the disabled employees the legislature requires that the only way to verify their professional and personal skills is probation for a period not exceeding 30 days. For this category of people skills verification by examination or interview is excluded, being in the presence of positive discrimination.

---

[42] Law no. 182/2002 on the protection of classified information, published in Official Gazette of Romania, part I, no. 248, April 12, 2002, with subsequent amendments

In the literature it said[43] that probation is optional and subsidiary to competition or examination. It is not assumed, nor is a unilateral act of the employer, but must be expressly provided for in the employment contract[44].

Establishment of the probationary period as a way of checking knowledge, unique or subsidiary to contest or examination is useful both for the employer and for the employee. Thus, the employer will better and directly appreciate employee competence and skills in the workplace, and may terminate the contract by giving notice, if the employee does not meet professional requirements. Probation is beneficial to the employee as well, as it provides the opportunity to see if the employee suits the assigned work. Currently, under art. 31 para. 4 of the Labor Code during the probationary period or at the end of it, the individual employment contract may be terminated by a simple written notice of either party.

Practical application of article 32 can cause certain problems, because the question refers to the status of the employee that will not be appropriate in the new position, but who is suitable for the position held prior to starting in the new profession. In our opinion, the type of work once modified in the individual employment contract, a change made with the employee's consent - in case the professional requirements of the new position are not met - the solution is the same, that is, dismissal without notice. But nothing prevents the contracting parties from establishing other terms, more favorable to the employee in such a situation.

---

[43] Al. Țiclea, Contractul individual de muncă, Lumina Lex Publishing House, București, 2003, p. 94
[44] Ş. Beligrădeanu, I.T. Ştefănescu, Perioada de probă în reglementarea Codului muncii, in „Dreptul" no. 8/2003, p. 25-26; I.T. Ştefănescu,Tratat de dreptul muncii, Wolters Kluwer Publishing House, București, 2007, p. 237 and the following;

The period in which more people can be successively employed on probation for the same job is 12 months (Article 33
Labor Code), the upper limit imposed by legislators is designed to prevent employers abuse the right to end unilaterally the individual labor contract during the probation period. The probationary period shall run and is calculated from
the first day of contract execution and it expires on its termination. During the probationary period the employee shall
enjoy all rights and have all obligations under applicable
rules of the employment contract, the period being considered seniority and length of service in social security systems.
Probation is, therefore, the period when employee skills and
professional training for performing that job are checked in
order to achieve the purpose for which the employment contract was concluded.

V.   Education and work experience conditions

For hiring and promotion in any position fulfillment of certain
conditions is required, such as education conditions, or training conditions for workers[45].

Hiring and promotion are subject to whether the conditions
of professional conduct are met. This is in consistency with
the necessity for an efficient and cost-effective activity for
each employer.

Theoretical and practical training, as well as the continuous
improvement, are a prerequisite to employment and promotion in work for all categories of employers. It is mandatory
for public sector units and has a character of recommendation, mainly to private sector units. However, there are situa-

---

[45] See I.T. Ştefănescu, Condiţii de studii şi verificarea lor, in „Raporturi de muncă" no.
5/1997, p. 47-50

tions where the law requires mandatory professional training for workers in this sector as well.

The nature and level of education for each occupation are designed directly related to the specialty and complexity of work, to duties and responsibilities involved in carrying it[46]. It should be noted that non-compliance of education conditions at the conclusion of the individual labor contract, when they are mandatory, shall be sanctioned with nullity, because a mandatory requirement, crucial to the very existence of the legal act in question is violated.

For compliance with certain functions or positions it is sometimes necessary that the future employee has, besides the necessary training, some occupational experience, and often some experience related to the specialized training required for the job in question.

According to Article 16 (3) of the Labor Code seniority is conferred to the employee who performs work under an employment contract, regardless of its form. In legal literature[47] it was stated that, broadly, seniority shall mean all periods for which a person has carried out activities under a typical or an atypical employment relationship. The rule is that, for seniority, periods during which the person was employed under an employment contract are considered.

Exceptionally, other time periods covered by the law, in which the person performed activities in independent or self-employed professions, count as seniority. This is possible on the premise that acquiring experience in exercising an occupation is accomplished by providing actual work, regardless of the nature of the legal relationship under which the work

---

[46] Al. Țiclea, Tratat de dreptul muncii, Rosetti Publishing House, București, 2006, p. 84
[47] V. Pătulea, Conținutul conceptului de „vechime în muncă", in „Dreptul" no. 2/2000, p. 82

was performed. In this sense, specialty seniority was defined[48] in the doctrine as the length of time a person has worked in activities corresponding to the position (job) in which they are to be employed or promoted. In the public sector laws governing performance of the activity usually require seniority conditions both for employment and promotion. Thus, in the case of judges, doctors, teachers, members of the Diplomatic and Consular Corps, civil service workers, specialty seniority conditions are provided for each function in the functional hierarchy by their personnel status.

In practice, both in the public sector and the private sector, employers include requirements for seniority in employment or in the profession, along with training conditions, as well as professional qualifications conditions. This reality is based on the fact that work experience has a positive effect on how the employee fulfills the primary obligation assumed by the individual labor contract. Thus, professionally, exercising the same profession for a period of time is reflected in the quality of work. From the point of view of management, however, exercising different occupations that require the same specialized studies is beneficial for the employee, who benefits from a wider scope, increased coverage and coordination of the activities performed.

In conclusion, it is to be noted that in Romania, which is still in a period of labor market dynamics, seniority is a reality born from the relationship between supply and demand on the labor market. This relationship favors job offers for staff with certain professional training and is unfavorable for individuals lacking professional qualifications or work experience.

---

[48] Al. Ţiclea, Tratat de dreptul muncii, Rosetti Publishing House, Bucureşti, 2006, p. 87

Title III
Rights And Obligations Of The Parties Of The Individual Employment Contract

Chapter 1
Contents Of The Individual Employment Contract

The content of the individual employment contract includes general rights and obligations of the parties. Thus, the employer is bound to ensure the provision of the agreed activities and also provide the employee with the means to perform it. He is obliged to pay the agreed salary ensure that the employee receives all the social benefits provided by law and by collective bargaining. He must also respect the professional qualifications agreed with the employee and not assign tasks that do not meet these qualifications. The employer must respect the dignity and privacy of the employee. In turn, the employee must perform work personally, he cannot be substituted by a third party in order to carry out the work in a conscientious and loyal manner, and he must be loyal to the employer. Being in a subordinate position, the employee shall obey orders and instructions of the employer, he shall comply with internal regulations, refrain from any act of competition, directly or indirectly, to the employer.

The main duties of the employees, mentioned in art. 39 para. 1 of the Labor Code are: entitlement to remuneration for their work, the right to benefit from daily and weekly rest, the right to have an annual leave, entitlement to equal treatment, the right to have dignity at work, the right to

health and safety, access to training, information and consultation rights, the right to take part in the determination and improvement of working conditions and the working environment, the right of protection in case of dismissal, the right to collective and individual bargaining, the right to participate in collective actions, the right to form or join a union. Most of these rights have constitutional protection as well.

The main obligations of employees are listed in art. 39 para. 2 of the Labor Code. These obligations are as follows: the obligation to respect the time required to perform the job or, if necessary, to fulfill the tasks assigned by the job description, the obligation to respect work discipline, the obligation to observe the provisions of the applicable collective agreement, as well as of the employment contract, the obligation of loyalty towards the employer in the performance of duties, the obligation to comply with health and safety measures in the work unit, and the obligation to observe secrecy.

The Labor Code also lists the basic rights of the employer under their contractual relationship with the employee namely: to establish the organization and operation of the firm, to establish suitable tasks for each employee, to give legal instructions to the employee, to exercise control over the performance of the employee's duties, to assess the disciplinary offenses and apply appropriate sanctions under the law, under the applicable collective agreement and under the internal regulations, to establish performance targets for employees and also their achievement benchmarks.

The Labor Code also establishes in art. 40 para. 2 the main obligations of the employer, namely: to inform employees of the conditions of work and on issues related to employment relationships, to ensure the ongoing technical and organizational conditions considered in the development of appropriate labor standards and working conditions, to respect all employee rights under the law, under the applicable collective agreement and under the individual employment contracts, to regularly communicate the economic and financial situation of the unit to the employees, to consult with the union or, where appropriate, with representatives of employees on decisions likely to affect substantially the employee rights and interests, to pay all their contributions and taxes, and to withhold and remit employee contributions and taxes due under the law, to establish the electronic register of employees and operate electronic records provided by law, to release upon request, all documents evidencing that the applicant is an employee, to ensure the confidentiality of employees 'personal data.

Besides the general clauses of the individual employment contract, the contents of the parties may include specific clauses, some of them being covered by the Labor Code, other by special laws.

The Labor Code illustrates in art. 20 four specific causes that can be negotiated by the parties and stipulated in the individual employment contract, namely: the clause on training, the non-compete clause, the mobility clause and the confidentiality clause.

I. The non-compete clause

The non-compete clause can be either negotiated on concluding the individual employment contract or during its execution. It consists, on the one hand, in the obligation of the employee, after the termination of the individual employment contract, not to provide, for themselves or for a third party, an activity that is in competition with that performed for their employer and. On the other hand, it refers to the employer's obligation to pay the employee for the entire period of prohibition a sum of money as compensation to limit the right to work.

II.   The mobility clause

The mobility clause is the clause in which the parties to the employment contract provide that, in consideration of the specific work, service obligations execution by the employee is not done in a stable workplace. From the wording of the text it is considered that the mobility provided by the Romanian legislator is a geographical and not a professional one. The mobility clause is different from the delegation, as a change of work place. In the case of delegation, changing the workplace is exceptionally imposed unilaterally by the employer, while in the case of the mobility clause; the rule is the mobility itself.

III.   The confidentiality clause

provided in art. 26 of the Labor Code is the clause whereby the parties agree that on the duration of the contract and after its termination they shall not transmit data or information which they acquired during the execution of the individual employment contract, within the conditions set out in the internal regulations, collective agreements or individual employment contracts. Data confidentiality must be ensured by both the employer and the employee. The employer has by law (art. 40 para. 2 of the Labor Code) the obligation to ensure the confidentiality of personal data of employees. The confidentiality clause has no legal time limit to be imposed after the individual employment contract termination.

IV.   The clause on training

The clause on training may be negotiated between the parties of the individual employment contract by detailing how to train the employee, beyond what is required by law. When such a clause is not negotiable, training of employees shall fall within those clauses specified in the Labor Code, in the applicable collective agreement or in internal rules.

By this specific clause the parties clearly determine the training method and the rights and obligations related to this clause, which are subject to the addenda of the individual employment contract.

Chapter 2
The Basic Rights Of The Employer And The Employee

The employee performs work under the authority of the employer, who has the power to give orders and directives to the employee, to control fulfillment of duties and penalize deviations from the work discipline. It is what is called legal subordination.

By concluding he individual employment contract, the employee is subordinated to the employers economically as well, as a consequence of the employee's main purpose, that is, to obtain an income that would ensure his family's and his own existence.

The powers of the employer may not, however, be exercised in an arbitrary manner, being limited by the content of the individual work contract, as well as by the mandatory rules of labor law.

I. The employer's right to organize the work of the firm

This right stems from the freedom to conduct a business recognized by art. 16 of the Charter of Fundamental Rights of the European Union. Thus, the employer invests capital and therefore he decides which is the activity of the firm, its purpose and resources necessary for this purpose, in which human resources have an important role.

It is undeniable therefore that the employer's authority involves organization of the firm, including employee labor organization by setting individual tasks in the job description
attached to the employment contract, but this power is not
absolute. The employer must exercise his rights in good faith,
in the interests of the entity that he controls. The employer's
decisions are sometimes conditioned, according to law, by a
certain preliminary procedure and they are always likely to
be subject to judicial review, both from the perspective of
their legality and of their solidity. Therefore, legislature has
determined that, on some important decisions regarding the
activity organization, such as those relating to labor standards, to the training of employees, to collective redundancies, the employer must consult in advance with trade unions
or representatives of employees.

The organizational prerogative of the employer cannot be
exercised in an exclusively subjective manner. Therefore, the
employer must, according to art. 40 para. 2 of the Labor
Code, regularly communicate the economic and financial
situation of the unit to workers.

Moreover, employer's decisions on the organization of work
activities, that have an impact on employees' rights, can be
subject to judicial review, the court having jurisdiction to determine whether the employer has improperly exercised authority in this regard.

II.   The right of the employer to issue directives regarding the employee activity

The authority of the employer must be known by the employee, the latter having the right to be made aware which are
the job duties and the rules governing the individual employment relationship, in the context of developing it within a

group. As a result, the power of the employer to issue directives, part of his authority to the employee, is reflected in the
employer's right to determine the tasks of each employee
and to establish rules of labor discipline, performing a regulatory action on the legal work relationship.

The attribute of the employer to issue directives on the work
of the employees must be exercised only by respecting the
principle of dignity at work of the employees, the principle of
non-discrimination of employees and that of keeping them
informed.

The employer is obliged to respect the equal treatment of all
employees, he shall not discriminate employees directly or
indirectly on the grounds of sex, sexual orientation, genetic
characteristics, age, nationality, race, color, ethnicity, religion, political views, social origin, disability, family status or
responsibilities, trade union activity or affiliation.

The power of the employer to issue directives is manifested
both in relation to the entire team of the firm and in relation
to each employee. Thus, the employer is obliged to draw up
internal rules containing normative provisions on individual
and collective labor relations, arrangements to be made
known to employees in order to become mandatory.

The employer must also prepare each employee's job description, establishing duties and responsibilities as well as
functional and hierarchical relationships within the institutional organization.

The employer has the right to give written and oral instructions about the development of work activity of the employee, subject to their legality, the employee not having the
right to refuse to fulfill them, even if considered to be inap-
propriate.

III. The employer's right to control the employee's work, to find and punish misbehavior

The employer has the right to control, inspect and monitor how employees comply with his activity organization provisions. However, in the case of the rights of the employer, it is important to relate to the nature of the subordinate employee benefits.

According to paragraph 40 1 letter d) of the Labor Code, the employer's right to control is exercised over the employee during the execution of the individual employment contract, but it is not unlimited. The employee is required to comply with both obligations expressly provided by law, by the applicable collective agreement, by the individual employment contract and also by orders given by the employer exercising his right to direct and organize the activity. By having the power to control, the employer verifies how the employee meets all these requirements. If, after exercising control, the employer establishes that the employee has violated labor discipline, he is entitled to apply, where appropriate, disciplinary actions.

IV. The employee's right to receive wages

The most important right of the employee is to receive wages.

Wages represent the consideration for the employee's work under the individual employment contract, being an essential element of the employment contract, the principal purpose for which the employee accepts to conclude te contract and to perform the required work.

The wages include the following elements: the base salary, allowances, bonuses and other benefits.

Wage determination, whether it is the result of individual or collective negotiation, or it is regulated by law, is governed by a set of principles, of which the following will be highlighted:

a. The principle of equal treatment;

b. The principle of establishing wages and of payment of wages in cash;

c. The principle of salary confidentiality;

d. The principle of establishing wages by negotiation;

e. The principle of guaranteeing the payment of the national minimum gross wages.

Title IV
Modification, suspension and termination of the individual employment contract

Chapter 1
Changing The Individual Employment Contract

Governed by Title II, Chapter III of the Labor Code, changing the individual employment contract is governed by the principle of the agreement of the Contracting Parties. There are, depending on the declaration of intent of the Contracting Parties, two forms of changing in the individual employment contract, namely:

a) Modification of the individual employment contract by agreement of the Contracting Parties;

b) Unilateral modification of the individual employment contract.

I.   Modification by agreement of the parties

In accordance with Directive 91/533/EEC, the Labor Code regulates the obligation of the employer to inform the employee on the provisions he intends to change. Changing one of the essential elements of the individual employment contract requires the completion of an addendum to the contract, within 20 days from the date of the written notice to the employee. Regarding the form of this act, it must be written, without it the addendum being void. The ascertainment of the individual work contract modification as a result of law provisions or unilaterally does not require

the conclusion of such an act. Regarding the amendment of the individual work contract, art. 41 para. 3 of the Labor Code states that the following are subject to change: duration of contract, type of work, working conditions, wages, working time and rest time, without the listing of these clauses being exhaustive.

III. Unilateral modification of the individual employment contract initiated by the employer

The current Labor Code regulates the delegation and job relocation. Unilateral changes in individual employment contract are temporary; they belong to the employer, who can decide, in the case of delegation and job relocation, only to change the work place, all other elements of the individual employment contract being amended only with the consent of the employee.

II.1. Delegation

Delegation is a way of changing unilaterally the individual employment contract. It refers to the employee temporarily performing his duties, as required by the employer, outside his workplace.

The delegation may be imposed for a period not exceeding 60 days in a calendar year and may be extended with the consent of the employee, with successive periods not exceeding 60 days. It is ordered by the employee in their own interest, thereby changing the employee's work place.

The delegated employee is entitled to receive payment for travelling and accommodation and an allowance of delegation, as provided by law or by the applicable collective bargaining agreement.

The employee shall retain his title or position and all the other rights under the contract.

II.2. Job relocation

Jobrelocation is the act that stipulates the temporary change of work place, from the employer's disposal, to another employer, for the execution of tasks in the interests of the latter. Exceptionally, by job relocation the type of work can be changed, only with written consent of the employee. Job relocation may be imposed for a period of maximum one year.

Still exceptionally, job relocation duration may be repeatedly extended for objective reasons which require the presence of the employee to the employer where he is relocated, with the agreement of both parties, once in 6 months. Also, the seconded employee may refuse job relocation for strong reasons such as his health state, special family situations, etc.

During job relocation the seconded employee enjoys all his rights, having the privilege of benefiting from the most favorable rights, that is, either those from the seconding employer or from the original employer.

If the seconding employer does not fulfill all obligations in full and on time to the seconded employee, these obligations will be met by the original employer.

Chapter 2
Suspension Of The Individual Employment Contract

Suspension of the individual employment contract finds itself - contained regulation in the current Labor Code, art. 49-54.

In a terse statement, suspending the individual employment contract means temporarily stopping the main effects of the individual employment contract, that is: work performed by the employee and the employee wages paid by the employer. Obviously, not all situations in which cessation of obligations of the parties occurs temporarily are situations of suspension of the individual employment contract. According to the law, the following types of suspension can be distinguished:

- *Suspension de jure;*

- *Suspension on the parties' agreement;*

- *Suspension on the employer's initiative;*

- *Suspension on the employee's initiative.*

I. Suspension de jure of the individual employment contract

Suspension *de jure* of the individual employment contract occurs by operation of law for reasons that are beyond the control of the contracting parties.

These reasons make it impossible to continue work provision, with a direct effect on the employer's obligation to pay wages.

The individual employment contract is suspended de jure in the following cases (Article 50 Labor Code):

a. Maternity leave;

b. Temporary disability leave;

c. Quarantine;

d. Fulfillment of the compulsory military service;

e. Exercise of a function within an executive, legislative or judicial body, during the entire term, unless the law provides otherwise;

f. Employment in a paid trade union management position;

g. Force majeure;

h. When an employee is taken into preventive custody, under the terms of the Code of Criminal Procedure;

i. In other cases expressly provided for in the law.

a. Maternity leave is a cause that leads to the suspension of the individual employment contract due to the objective inability of the woman employed to provide the specific activity because of the situation caused by pregnancy and confinement.

b. Temporary disability leave is granted if, due to an accident at work or outside of work, to an occupational disease or a common one, the employee cannot provide objectively the specific work.

c. Quarantine is also a cause for suspension of the individual employment contract which leads to temporary cessation of work due to a contagious disease that would endanger the health or life of employees. Quarantine has the effect of suspending the individual employment contract with specific effects, namely: non-provision of work and unpaid wages.

d. Exercise of functions within an executive, legislative or judicial body, throughout the term of the contract involves the suspension of the individual employment contract during the entire term, unless overlapping of functions is allowed by a special law.

e. Employment in a paid trade union management position also causes the suspension de jure of the individual employment contract.

f. Force majeure and fortuitous event have the same effect on the two essential elements of the individual employment contract.

g. If the employee is taken into custody, according to the Code of Criminal Procedure, the individual employment contract is suspended, as in the case of employee participation in a strike, due to the fact that no work is performed and there is no paid salary for the period of temporary interruption.

III. Suspension of the individual employment contract by agreement of the parties

The individual employment contract may be suspended by agreement, in the case of unpaid leave for study or personal interests.

IV. Suspension of the individual employment contract on the initiative of the employer

The individual employment contract is suspended on the initiative of the employer in the following cases:

a. during the preliminary disciplinary hearing, under the terms of the law;

b. as a disciplinary sanction;

c. when the employer has lodged a criminal complaint against the employee or he was prosecuted for criminal acts incompatible with the position held, until a final judgment has been issued;

d. in case of temporary interruption of the activity, without a cessation of the employment relationship, in particular for economic, technological, structural or similar reasons;

e. during the job relocation or posting.

V. Suspension of the individual employment contract on the employee's initiative

The individual employment contract may be suspended on the initiative of the employee, in the following situations, expressing their wish to do so (Article 51 Labour Code):

a. parental leave for children;

b. leave for care of sick child under the age of seven years or, in the case of a disabled child, for intercurrent diseases, up to the age of eighteen years;

c. paternity leave;

d. vocational training leave;

e. exercise of elective offices within professional bodies established at central or local level, during the entire term;

a. The parental leave shall be granted to policy holders who benefited from income subject to income tax in the last 12 months preceding the date of birth of the child.

Recepients can choose between different leave periods, ie until the child is 1 year or 2 years, and in the case of disabled children up to the age of 3 years.

b. The leave for care of sick child under the age of seven years or, in the case of a disabled child, for intercurrent diseases, up to the age of 18 years shall be granted throughout the suspension, policy holders benefiting from an allowance which is fully supported by the National Fund of health insurance. The length of the allowance is 45 days per year for a child, unless the child is diagnosed with certain disorders set by law.

c. The paternity leave is granted to the father for a period of 5-10 working days. The parental leave is granted on request, in the first 8 weeks from childbirth, supported by his birth certificate, which shows the quality of the father of the petitioner. The allowance for paternity leave is paid from the payroll of the firm and it equals the wage of the corresponding period.

d. The training leave is another cause for suspension of the individual employment contract on the initiative of the employee, who may benefit from an application for leave with or without pay, in order to participate in training programs that fall under the job description of the position they hold.

e. The exercise of elective offices within professional bodies established at central or local level, during the entire term is still a cause for suspension of the individual employment contract employee's initiative.

Chapter 3
Termination Of The Individual Employment Contract

The individual employment contract can be terminated de jure, after agreement of the parties or after the unilateral initiative of one of the parties in the cases and under the terms restrictively provided for in the law.

I. Termination de jure of the individual employment contract

The individual employment contract is terminated de jure, that is, by law, when there has been a particular cause, expressly established by law, which makes producing further effects of the contract definitively impossible.

According to art. 56 of the Labor Code the employment contract ceases de jure:

- on the date of employee death;

- on the date of the final judgment certifying the death or legal guardianship of the employee;

- on the date the decision of employee old-age retirement, full or partial early retirement or invalidity retirement has been notified according to the law;

- following the establishment of the absolute nullity of the individual employment contract, from the date the nullity was established by agreement of the parties or by final judgment;

- when the demand of reinstatement in the position held by a person unlawfully or groundlessly dismissed has been admitted, from the date of the final reinstatement judgment;

- following the conviction to a prison term, from the date of the final judgment;

- from the date the competent authorities or bodies withdraw the approvals, authorizations or attestations necessary for the exercise of the profession;

- following the interdiction to practice a profession or a function, as a safety measure or complementary punishment, from the date of the final interdiction judgment;

- at the end of the individual employment contract of limited duration;

- following the withdrawal of the agreement of the parents or legal representatives, for the employees from fifteen to sixteen years old.

II. Termination of the individual employment contract by the agreement of the parties

The irrevocability principle can be defined as the rule of law according to which conventions can not be put an end by the unilateral will of either party. Irrevocability is a consequence and, at the same time, a guarantee of the principle of the compulsory nature of the contract.

As with other contracts, the individual employment contract may be terminated by agreement of the two parties. The Labor Code does not provide any conditions for the procedure or form of this agreement, allowing the contracting parties to regulate the concrete manifestation of the will agreement to end the employment relationship.

III. Resignation - termination of the individual employment contract on the employee's unilateral initiative

Not only the employer, but also the employee has the possibility of unilateral termination of the individual employment contract, as a consequence of the principle of freedom of labor.

The Labour Code defines resignation in art. 81 para. 1 as the unilateral act of the employee who, by a written notification, communicates the employer the cessation of the individual employment contract at the end of the notice period. Lack of written notification does not result in nullity of the resignation, the document is only a condition of evidence and not resignation validity.

The conditions under which the employee may take the initiative of termination of the employment contract by resignation are referred to in para. 2 - 7 of the same article and include the notice period, the situation of the employment contract during the notice period, the date of termination of employment, and the right of the employee not to motivate his resignation.

As a result of the resignation being a unilateral and irrevocable act, after the employer has been notified, the employee can not return to his manifestation of will. If the employer agrees, however, expressly or impliedly, the employee may waive the resignation, the employment contract continuing to have legal effect.

V.   Dismissal - termination of the employment contract on the employer's initiative

To ensure stability in the work of the employees, the Labor Code regulates expressly the grounds on which the employer may terminate the employment contract by his unilateral initiative.

Dismissal may occur for reasons related to the employee or for reasons not related to him, according to art. 58 para. 2 of the Labor Code.

V.1.   The dismissal for reasons related to the person of the employee

In art. 61 of the Labor Code the cases in which the employer may decide the dismissal for reasons related to the employee are listed as follows:

- when the employee has committed a serious or repeated disciplinary offence related to the labour discipline rules or the rules laid down in the individual employment contract, applicable collective labour agreement or rules of procedure, as a disciplinary sanction;

- when the employee has been taken into preventive custody for more than 30 days, under the terms of the Code of Criminal Procedure;

- when, by decision of the competent medical examination bodies, a physical and/or mental inability of the employee is found, not allowing him/her to fulfil the duties corresponding to the position held;

- when the employee is not professionally fit to the workplace where he/she is employed.

To avoid abuses of employers regarding dismissal, both for reasons related to the employee, but also for reasons unrelated to him, in order to ensure stability in the work of employees and to respect their rights of defense, the Labor Code includes several rules to be followed in such cases. These rules refer to prohibition of dismissal, the procedure for taking the measure and legality of dismissal. The provisions of art. 59 and art. 60 para.1 establish that dismissal is prohibited as follows:

- based on sex, sexual orientation, genetic characteristics, age, national affiliation, race, colour, ethnicity, religion, political option, social origin, disability, family situation or responsibility, trade union affiliation or activity;

- based on the exercise, under the terms of the law, of the right to strike and to unionisation;

- during the temporary disability, as certified by a medical certificate according to the law;

- during the quarantine leave;

- during the pregnancy of the employee, insofar as the employer took knowledge of it prior to issuing the dismissal decision;

- during the maternity leave;

- during the parental leave for children under two years of
age or, in the case of a disabled child, up to the age of
three years;

- during the parental leave for children under seven years of
age or in the case of a disabled child, for intercurrent diseases, up to the age of eighteen years;

- during the exercise of an elective office in a trade union,
except for the case where the dismissal is decided for serious
or repeated disciplinary offences of that employee;

- during the leave.

With respect to procedural rules, the Labor Code imposes
preliminary investigation before the disciplinary dismissal and
prior assessment of the employee in the case of professional
nonconformity. Moreover, the obligation to notify the other
party of the individual employment contract termination is
expressly provided for in the Labor Code. The aim is to avoid
the negative consequences that could occur in the case of
unilateral termination of the contract for the employee and it
represents a guarantee of the right to work and of employment stability. In the case of collective redundancies legislature requires a special procedure, which includes informing
the public authorities about this situation.

Regardless of the reasons underlying the dismissal, not inherent or inherent to the employee, legality control of this mode
of termination of the individual employment contract, is the
obligation of the courts, financially and territorrially competent to hear conflicts of rights. The legislature establishes that

any dismissal ordered by non statutory procedure is null and void.

The legal work relationships are regulated by the Labor Code, by other regulatory legal acts regarding work relationships and by collective labor contracts. These regulations establish the minimum rights and duties of the parties of the legal work relationship that must be complied with by both employer and employee.

They also establish the substance and the form conditions of the conclusion, performance and termination of employment contracts and the settlement rules for disputes which may arise in connection with the development of legal work relationships.

Legal regulations aimed at ensuring the stability of legal work relationships defend the legitimate interests of both employees and employers. Determination of cases and legal reasons for termination of employment as a unilateral initiative of the employer is the most important guarantee for the right to work. Terms of form and content of the act by which the employer shall terminate the employment contract are required by law to prevent possible abuses of employers and to have enough information to verify the legality and grounds of any measure ordered. These demands are justified, especially in cases where termination of legal employment occurs as a disciplinary sanction measure.

V.2.   Dismissal for reasons unrelated to the employee

Article 65 of the Labor Code regulates dismissal for reasons unrelated to the employee, due to the elimination of the position held by the employee for one or more reasons not related to his person. The condition that must be met for a dismissal to be lawful is the effective elimination of the workplace, based on a real and serious cause. The elimination of the workplace is effective when the workplace is suppressed from the organizational strucutre of the employer.

To find this, the positions of the employer's organization are to be investigated. The elimination of the workplace has a real cause when it is objective, being imposed by economic difficulties or technological changes. It is serious when it is based on thorough studies aimed at improving the work and when it does not conceal reality.

V.3. Collective dismissal

The Labor Code considers particularly important cases when dismissal for reasons not related to the employee affects more employees within a period of 30 days. Legislature regulates in detail the situation, putting into internal law the union law provisions.

In the current wording of art. 68 of the Labor Code, the Romanian legislator has opted for a literal transcription of the first option allowed by the Directive, namely dismissal in a period of 30 days of a number of:

-at least 10 employees, when the dismissing employer has more than 20 employees, but less than 100 employees;

-at least 10% of the employees, when the dismissing employer has at least 100 employees, but less than 300 employees;

- at least 30 employees, when the dismissing employer has at least 300 employees.

The procedure to be followed by the employer in order to make collective redundancies is strictly regulated by law, its violation resulting in invalidity of the measure, invalidity that can be determined by the court to settle a dispute against collective dismissal.

The measure of collective dismissal will result in a final dismissal of each employee. Thus, the employer shall, according to the principle of legal symmetry, establish in writing dismissal for each employee whose workplace is eliminated, resulting in the termination of the individual employment contract.

Title V
Types Of Individual Employment Contracts
Chapter 1

The Romanian Labor Code, which entered into force on March 1, 2003, approached the need for flexible types of contracts, covering the following types of employment contract:

- The employment contract concluded for an indefinite period;

- The employment contract concluded for a fixed period;

- The individual part-time employment contract;

- Temporary work agency employment;

- Work at home;

- Apprenticeship work contract.

Each of the above mentioned contract types has specific legal regulations that complement those applicable to the typical employment contract, to which the Labor Code allo-
cates most of its rules, which shows that, in general, the
characteristics of the standard individual labor contract are
also found in its atypical forms. To emphasize this, in what follows, each type of employment contract will be examined.

I.   The typical individual employment contract

The current legislation maintains, as a rule, concluding full-
time individual contracts of indefinite duration, where work is
provided in locations belonging to the employer. This regulation aims to legally protect an employee to whom this type
of legal work relationship provides stability.

The Labor Code in force exhaustively governs the institution
of the classic individual employment contract, to which it
devotes 69 articles. These articles contain provisions relating
to the conclusion, performance, amendment and termination
of the individual employment contract.

In order to clarify the various legal nuances of the typical
employment contract one must consider that its elements
should be reviewed, that is, the indefinite duration for which
it is concluded, the full time work and the work place.

I.1.   Indefinite duration

The indefinite duration of an individual employment contract
does not mean that it is completed by the appearance of
old age social risk but that the duration of that contract is
not known at the time concluded. As shown in the literature[49],

---

[49] E. Cristoforeanu, Teoria generală a contractului individual de muncă, Curierul
Judiciar Publishing House, București, 1937, p. 84

by the indefinite duration of the contract it should not be understood that the employee is required to work all his life for that employer or that the employer is required to keep the employee in service to death, but the duration is not known during the time the contract was concluded.

I.2. Full time employment

To qualify as typical employment contracts of indefinite duration a contract must be completed full-time, or for a full time job. The normal working hours for employees with labor contracts, according to art. 109, paragraph 1 of the Labor Code, are, on average, 8 hours per day and 40 hours a week. For young people aged up to 18 years working full time means, according to paragraph 2 of the same Article, 6 hours per day and 30 hours a week. Distribution of working hours in a week, according to art. 110, paragraph 1 is usually uniform, 8 hours per day for five days, two days of rest, the parties being able to opt for an unequal distribution in days subject to the limit of 40 hours a week.

I.3. The work place

A typical employment contract requires that the place of work belongs to the employer, who is obliged to provide the necessary working conditions for employees, according to his own rules set out in establishing and organizing documents and in internal regulations.

The number of typical employment contracts concluded for an indefinite period and full-time in our country is overwhelming.

Guide for Romanian and German Labour Law
Basics of the Employment Relationship

Measures to adapt to change in the labor market led to the appearance, besides the full-time work relationship with an indefinite duration, of other types of work relationships which are more flexible: fixed-term employment, part-time work, work at home and labor through temporary employment agency. These employment contracts are characterized by a decrease in the employee guarantees.

The need to make flexible forms of employment compatible, compatibility required by employers, with employee rights protection ensured, is the challenge that must be confronted by the social policy and labor legislation in the national law.

II.   The individual fixed-term employment contract

II.1.   The national regulation of the individual employment contract of limited duration

An employee with a fixed-term individual employment contract is the employee whose work contract is directly concluded with an employer. Termination of this contract is caused by objective conditions such as completion of the period on which it was concluded, the ending of the activity, service or production. Termination cannot be caused by the will of the contracting parties[50].

Regulation of the individual employment contract of limited duration conducted in the Labor Code deals with this type of

---

[50] See, on the analysis of this type of employment contract, I.T. Stefanescu, Ş. Beligrădeanu, Prezentare de ansamblu şi observaţii critice asupra noului Cod al muncii, in „Dreptul" no. 4/2003, p. 5 et seq.; Al. Athanasiu, L. Dima, Regimul juridic al raporturilor de muncă în reglementarea noului Cod al muncii, in „Pandectele române" no. 4/2003; I.T. Ştefănescu, Modificările Codului muncii comentate, edition 2005 and 2006, Lumina Lex Publishing House, Bucureşti; Al. Athanasiu, L. Dima, Dreptul muncii, All Beck Publishing House, Bucureşti, 2005, p. 58-59; Al. Ţiclea, Tratat de dreptul muncii, Rosetti Publishing House, Bucureşti, 2006, p. 365-369; I.T. Ştefănescu, Tratat de dreptul muncii, Wolters Kluwer Publishing House, Bucureşti, 2007, p. 403 et seq.; M. Volonciu, Comment (to art. 80-86) in Al. Athanasiu, M. Volonciu, L. Dima, O. Cazan Codul muncii, Comentariu pe articole, vol. I art. 1-107, C.H. Beck Publishing House, Bucureşti, 2007, p. 424 et seq.

contract as an exception to the rule of conclusion of permanent and full-time contracts. The material is included in art. 82-87 reprinted in the Labor Code.

According to art. 83 of the Labor Code, cases where fixed-term employment contracts may be concluded are exhaustively and expressly provided, as follows:

- To replace an employee on account of suspension of his contract, unless that employee participates in a strike. This is the so-called replacement contract or interim agreement in other legislation and it proved an effective means of creating and distributing jobs where an employee has the right to suspend the employment contract under the laws and under the collective agreement;

- For growth and/or temporary change of the activity structure of the unit; the contract is called in other legislations contract for production reasons. These reasons, be it an unexpected number of orders or unusual reasons such as excessive absenteeism, preclude the possibility of the employer to meet production requirements;

- For development of seasonal activities, the contract is designed especially for agricultural campaigns;

- To temporarily favor certain categories of unemployed persons, under legal provisions issued for this purpose;

- To employ a person seeking a job, that within 5 years from the date of employment qualifies for old-age pension;

- To fill an eligible positions in trade unions and NGOs during the mandate;

- For employing pensioners who, under the law, can benefit from both salary and pension;

- In other cases expressly provided for by special laws, or for performing different projects or programs.

The maximum period for which an employment contract of limited duration may be concluded is 36 months. The parties may also conclude the contract for a shorter period and extend it within the maximum of 36 months, with no limit to the number of extensions.

An individual labor contract extension must take place before the expiry of the original period for which the contract was concluded, because the individual employment contract is terminated at this time and, therefore, it cannot be extended since it is no longer valid.

During the 36 months, between the same parties, that is, employer and employee, no more than three successive fixed-term contracts can be concluded. Thus, if the employer has concluded an individual contract of employment with a person for a period of 2 months for the execution of certain work, they may conclude other two contracts with the same person, up to the maximum period of 36 months. One must consider as successive only fixed-term contracts whose duration cannot be longer than 12 months, without a break longer than three months between the first termination date and the date of conclusion of the next contract.

The individual fixed-term employment contract is concluded in written form, according to art. 82 para. 2 of the Labor Code. The content of the individual labor contract was approved by Ministry of Labor Order no. 64/2003, amended by Ministry of Labor Order no. 76/2003 and Order no. 1616/2011. It includes minimal provisions, and can be adapted to each type of employment contract. Obligation to register individual employment contracts in special registers for recording employees applies for any type of employment contract.

The fixed-term individual employment contract follows the same rules and procedures for conclusion in writing and for recording as the indefinite contract.

Moreover, according to art. 87 para. 1 of the Labor Code, employees with fixed-term individual employment contracts will not be treated less favorably than comparable permanent employees, in terms of employment and working conditions, unless different treatment is justified on objective grounds.

A comparable permanent employee' refers to the employee whose individual employment contract is concluded for an indefinite period and who performs the same or a similar activity in the same unit, taking into account their qualifications, skills or training.

The fixed-term contract differs from the classical contract by conditions for termination, generally reaching the term and being terminated on the expiry date of the period for which it was concluded. Exceptionally, the employee may terminate the fixed-term contract, but only for justified reasons, which exclude his fault, otherwise risking paying some compensation to the employer for damages caused by improper exercise of his right to resign.

Limitations that the law requires for the conclusion of fixed-term employment contracts are intended to maintain the rule of conclusion of the indefinite duration employment contract. Thus, if the number of successive contracts had not been limited, one could notice some chain employment of the same employee. This chain employment is possible when each of the fixed-term contracts concluded by the same person has different objectives (e.g. replacement of the employee and fulfillment of a certain task).

II.2   Community legislation of the individual fixed term employment

For rules on the conclusion of fixed-term individual employment contracts the provisions of Directive 99/70/CE, referring to the Framework Agreement on fixed-term work concluded by ETUC, UNICE and CEEP[51]. The signatories of the Framework Agreement recognize that the contracts of indefinite duration are and remain the general form of labor relations between employers and employees, but admit that these fixed term contracts respond, in certain circumstances, to labor market needs.

Clause 4 of the Framework Agreement establishes the principle of non-discrimination, whereby workers with fixed-term contracts should not be treated differently from comparable workers with employment contracts concluded for an indefinite period, except to the extent that such different treatment is justified on objective grounds.

The Agreement establishes the general principles and minimum requirements relating to fixed-term work, recognizing that for their implementation one must consider realities of national, sectorial and seasonal situations. The main concern of the Community institutions and of the European social partners was to establish a framework that would ensure equal treatment and non-discrimination of employees with fixed-term contracts, protecting them against discrimination, given that more than half of those who signed these contracts are women.

The agreement applies to community employees who have a fixed term employment contract, excluding jobs available to

---

[51] Directive 99/70/CE of 28 June 1999, concerning the framework agreement on fixed-term work concluded by ETUC, UNICE and CEEP, published in Official Journal of European Union, Series L 175, July 10, 1999

a company through a temporary work agency, and is capable of not being applied to employment contracts of apprenticeship if so decided by the Member States and by the social partners.

According to clause no. 3 of the Agreement, the employee with the fixed term contract means 'an employee with an employment contract or employment relationship concluded directly between an employer and an employee, when the termination of work or employment relationship is caused by objective conditions such as the established date, completion of the activity or service or of production'.

Thus, as the intention of the Directive is to prevent discrimination, it establishes the concept of comparable employee with permanent contract, that is, 'an employee with a contract or employment relationship of indefinite duration, in the same unit, which performs work or an activity that is identical or similar, given their qualifications and the tasks they perform', and emphasizes that 'if there is no comparable permanent employee during the same unit, the comparison shall be made with reference to the collective agreement applicable or, where there is no applicable collective agreement, in accordance with legislation, collective agreements or practice'.

In conclusion, the objectives of the Community Directive on fixed-term employment contracts are to create jobs, to avoid discrimination and differentiation between employees with employment contracts of indefinite duration and those with fixed-term employment contracts and also avoid abuse of the employer in the use of this type of contract. These objectives should, in principle, be reflected in the national legislation of Romania, as a Member State of the European Union.

III. The individual part-time employment contract

III.1. Regulation of the individual part-time employment contract in law

The Labor Code expressly governs, for the first time, the individual part-time employment contract as a distinct type of employment contract, which can be concluded both permanently and on a fixed-term. This new regulation of the Romanian law considered the provisions of Council Directive 97/81/EC concerning the EU Framework Agreement on part-time work[52], agreement concluded between organizations representing employers and employees at Community level[53].

In its current form art. 103 defines the part-time employee as the employee whose normal number of hours of work, calculated weekly or as a monthly average, is lower than the number of normal working hours of a comparable full-time employee. The solution currently adopted by the legislature is not the most appropriate. Thus, the absence of legal limits of working time for an activity - the object of the individual employment contract - creates a lot of confusion in practice.

The Labor Code defines the comparable employee as a full-time employee in the same unit, with the same type of activity or one similar to that of the employee with a part-time employment contract, taking into account other considerations, such as seniority and qualification, or professional skills.

The individual part-time employment contract must specify, in addition to the specific terms of any employment contract, details of work duration and distribution of working hours, conditions that can change working hours and the interdic-

---

[52] Council Directive 97/81/EC of 15 December 1997 concerning the EU Framework Agreement on part-time work, published in Official Journal of the European Union, Series L 014, January 20,1998

[53] See Code de droit social europeen Litec Publishing House, Paris, 2002, p. 440-445

tion of working overtime - except in cases of force majeure or for other urgent works aimed at preventing accidents and eliminating their consequences (art. 105 para. 1).

The employee with a part-time employment contract shall enjoy all the rights of full-time employees, as determined by law and by applicable collective agreements. The remuneration shall be paid according to the time actually worked by the principle of *pro rata*. Other rights, such as annual leave, seniority, and length of service in social security systems are fully granted to part-time employees.

The Labor Code, art. 107 para. 3 sets the employer's obligation to provide access to part-time contracts for all staff in the organization, which means that the management positions may also be filled by employees with part-time individual employment contracts. Part-time jobs are set by the employer, the employee having the right to ask their employer to be switched to part-time work, and, if he agrees, to amend the employment contract in terms of normal working time.

Also in the Romanian legislation, similar to other EU legislation some formal requirements are set for this type of contract conclusion. Thus, art. 104 para. 2 of the Labor Code requires the conclusion of a written part-time individual employment contract and art. 105 para. 1 states that the content of the contract should include, besides the essential elements of the contents of a typical employment contract, the following three elements:

a) Hours of work and distribution of working hours;

b) The conditions under which this distribution can be modified;

c) The interdiction of overtime work, except in cases of absolute necessity.

If these elements are not specified in the individual part-time employment contract, it is deemed to have been concluded for a full time, the contract not being void (art. 105 para. 2 of the Labor Code.) Accordingly, the written form of the individual part-time employment contract has an ad probationem value[54], which means that if the parties have not concluded it in writing, it shall be considered a full-time employment contract, unless the parties prove the contrary. In theory opinions have been expressed that the written form of a part-time contract would be a condition of validity[55].

Breach of art. 105 para. 2 does not void the contract, but only changes its legal classification, at the request of the employee, if he provided a full time work or if the employer cannot demonstrate the part-time work contract feature. There are no differences in terms of formal conditions compared with those of the individual full-time work contract. This contract is concluded according to the model approved by the Minister of Labor by Order no. 64/2003, and follows the same rules for registration as a typical contract.

Unlike regulations in different European countries, art. 105 para. 1 letter c) of the Labor Code sets the interdiction to work overtime for part-time employees, except in cases of force majeure or for other urgent works to prevent the occurrence of accidents or to eliminate their consequences. However, this is a restrictive regulation that may adversely affect

---

[54] I.T. Ştefănescu, Tratat de dreptul muncii, Wolters Kluwer Publishing House, Bucureşti, 2007, p. 423; M. Volonciu, Comment (to art. 101) in Al. Athanasiu, M. Volonciu, L. Dima, O. Cazan Codul muncii, Comentariu pe articole, vol. I art. 1-107, C.H. Beck Publishing House, Bucureşti, 2007, p. 524-525
[55] See Al. Ţiclea, Tratat de dreptul muncii, Rosetti Publishing House, Bucureşti, 2006, p. 529

the economic interests of the employer as well as employee interests. It would have been preferable for overtime to be capped at a certain level, or for greater flexibility in working time conditions to be permitted. This happens in other legislation, such as the Spanish, and the conditions are stipulated in the contract with a provision of the "overtime" that can be added to the normal working time, always taking into account the prior consent of the employee. The problem should be solved in the future by changing the law, with the purpose of introducing a maximum level for additional work that can be done by a part-time employee, level of work related to the total working hours negotiated.

III.2. Regulation of the part-time individual employment contract by Community law[56]

Part-time contract settlement in Community law was done specifically to encourage this form of contract as a means of creating new jobs. The framework Agreement on part-time work concluded between the Industry and Employers Confederations of Europe (UNICE), the European Trade Union Confederation (ETUC) and the European Centre of Enterprises with Public Participation (CEEP) is part of the overall strategy of employment within the Community, which aims to promote flexible working forms. The preamble to the Framework Agreement on part-time employment contracts underlines its aim to contribute to the overall European strategy for employment, as part-time work has an important impact on employment in recent years.

---

[56] Community rules analysis is based on information contained in selection Relații de muncă. Modul de curs, published by the Labor Inspection, Romania, Labor Inspection and Social Security, Spain, RO-03/IB/SO-01 PHARE Project, Oscar Print Publishing House, București, 2005, p. 80-88

According to clause 1 of Directive 97/81/EC[57] for implementations of the Framework Agreement on part-time work, closed between confederation-type organizations UNICE, CEEP and the ETUC, the objective of the Framework Agreement is[58]:

- To provide for the elimination of discrimination against part-time workers and to improve the quality of part-time work;

- To facilitate the development of part-time work on a voluntary basis and to contribute to the flexible organization of working time in a manner of considering the needs of employers and workers.

According to the second clause of the Directive, the scope of the Agreement extends for 'part-time employees who have a contract or employment relationship as defined in the legislation, in the collective agreements or by practices in force in each Member State'. 'Member States in consultation with social partners, in accordance with the national law, collective agreements or practice (and/or in consultation with the social partners at the relevant level in accordance with national industrial relations practices) could, for objective reasons, wholly or partly exclude the provisions of the Agreement for part-time employees who work occasionally. Despite these facts, these exclusions should be reviewed periodically to determine if the objective reasons that they support are valid.

Under clause 3 of the Agreement, part-time employees are those employees whose normal working day, calculated on a week or on an average of a maximum work period of 1 year, is shorter than the one of a comparable full-time employee.

---

[57] Published in Official Journal of the European Union, Series L 14, January 20, 1998
[58] A. Popescu, Dreptul internaţional al muncii, C.H. Beck Publishing House, Bucureşti 2006, p. 568

A comparable employee is a full-time employee in the same establishment having the same type of contract or employment relationship and the same or similar work, also with regard to other considerations such as seniority and qualifications or duties. If there is no comparable full-time employee in the same establishment, the comparison shall be made by reference to the applicable collective labor contract or, if there is no applicable collective labor contract, in accordance with law in collective agreements or practice.

Most European systems have adapted the concept of part-time work employee to the community directive, but there are laws that require the employee a maximum percentage of part-time hours as compared to the full-time employee (such as Portugal, asking for below 75%). Laws could, conversely, require a minimum of hours and days worked for considering such a contract (such as in the case of Greece).

In conclusion, the Framework Agreement on part time labor materializes the will of social partners to establish a general framework for eliminating discrimination on part-time workers, so as to create conditions for fostering conclusion of this type of employment contract to cover the needs labor market.

IV.   The individual work at home contract

IV.1.   Internal regulations on work at home contracts

Domestic work is regulated in art. 108-110 of the Labor Code as a means of enforcing individual permanent or temporary employment contracts, full-time or part-time, with the main feature that work is performed at the employee's home[59]. The labor code, when referring to work at home contracts, states

---

[59] I.T. Ştefănescu, Ş. Beligrădeanu, Prezentare de ansamblu şi observaţii critice asupra noului Cod al muncii, in „Dreptul" no. 4/2003, p. 54

that three specific clauses should be included in it, along with the mandatory elements that constitute the legal individual employment contract. These clauses are[60]:

- The explicit provision that the employee works at home;

- The program under which the employer has the right to control their employee activity and the concrete way of achieving control;

- The employer's obligation to provide transportation to and from the employee's residence for raw materials and materials that they use in their activity, and the finished products.

Article 106 of the Labor Code establishes the written form of the contract as a condition of probation, not of validity[61]. Work at home employees set their own work schedule, which may be different from that of the employer and fragmented during the working day.

Article 107 of the Labor Code provides that employee to work from home enjoys all rights stipulated by law and by collective bargaining agreements applicable to employees whose work place belongs to the employer.

Provisions contained in the Labor Code relating to work at home contracts, although brief, are, in principle, in accordance with regulations in other European countries in the same field, but are more restrictive. Thus, art. 105 para.1 of the Labor Code restricts the ability of the employee to perform the work at home only, while other legislation, including Convention 177/1996 on work at home of ILO, Convention non-ratified by our country, provide that work can be performed in another place determined by the employee, on

---

[60] O. Ţinca, Contractul individual de muncă la domiciliu, in „Dreptul" no. 8/2003, p. 34
[61] For an adverse opinion, see Al. Ţiclea, Tratat de dreptul muncii, Rosetti Publishing House, Bucureşti, 2006, p. 531

condition that it does not belong to the employer[62]. Romania's labor code provides no opportunity for employees to work at home to be helped by family members as required by regulations in other European countries. Internal regulations refer only to the employer's obligation to provide transportation of raw materials, but do not set anything on the employer bearing the expenditure that the employee makes at work. Also, none of the provisions of the Labor Code in connection with evidence that the employer must keep related to the work at home employee's activity. Of course the two parties can negotiate various additional clauses in the employment contract, but it is advisable that conducting labor relations based on employment contract – type documents would not be so general but specific, otherwise it may lead to abuses in practice, affecting the possibilities for action of justice and administration.

In conclusion, the work at home contract will gain an increasingly important role in the types of contracts, which will require more detailed regulation of contract terms, how to materialize the subordination of the employee to his employer.

IV.2. Community concerns related to work at home contracts[63]

In the European Union on 27 May 1998 the Commission adopted a Recommendation on the ratification of ILO Convention no. 177/1996 on work at home. The Commission stated that about 5% of the active population of the European

---

[62] O. Tinca, Contractul individual de muncă la domiciliu, in „Dreptul" no. 8/2003, p. 51
[63] Community rules analysis is based on a selection of information contained in Relaţii de muncă. Modul de curs, prepared by the Labour Inspection, Romania, Labour Inspection and Social Security, Spain, RO-03/IB/SO-01 PHARE Project, Oscar Print Publishing House, Bucureşti, 2005, p. 97-99

Union works at home, the majority being women. Convention ILO 177/1996 states that the term 'work at home' means work performed by a person at home or in another place chosen by them, outside the places owned by the employer, in order to accomplish a product or service that is in accordance to employer specifications.

Under the Convention the source of raw materials used in the work process is not important, but it is important that workers do not have the degree of autonomy and economic independence necessary to be considered independent workers under the national legislation or under judicial decisions.

According to art. 4 of the Convention ILO no. 177/1996, Member States which ratify it must promote equality of treatment between workers at home and other workers, in particular as regards:

- The right of workers at home to form or join organizations of their choice and participate in their activities;

- Protection against discrimination in employment and occupation;

- Protection of health and safety matters;

- Remuneration;

- Access to training;

- Minimum age of employment;

- Maternity.

This type of work at home contract is very common in countries like France, Britain and Italy, while in other countries like Greece, Spain and Portugal working from home is not rooted in formal terms and is even more often confused with authorized person, and even with forms of underground economy.

In Belgium, the home worker is one who, under the authority, but not directly under the supervision or control of the employer, performs work at home or at a place of his choice. In Switzerland, by the home employment contract, the employee is obliged to perform at home or another place of their choice, alone or with family members in exchange for a wage, a work for the employer.

Analysis of the Labor Code provisions relating to work at home highlights the fact that, as noted, they are restrictive to similar regulations in the Member States of the European Union, which have long experience in the labor market. Thus, art. 105 para. 1 of the Labor Code restricts performing activities only to work performed at the employee's home, while other legislation shall provide the possibility that labor is supplied in another place, provided it does not belong to the employer. Also, the Romanian legislation does not provide, compared with other legislation, the possibility for the employee to work at home to be helped by family members.

V.   Work through a temporary employment agency

The permanent and full-time work relationship has been largely replaced by other types of labor relationships that are more flexible: temporary employment, part-time work, temporary assignment, work at home and work through a temporary employment agency. All these types are part of what is called 'atypical work', which is characterized by a decrease in the level of security for employees and by reduction of union power.

The need to make the flexibility of employers compatible with the protection of workers' rights was and is still the challenge that social policies and labor law must confront. In this context, the use of a temporary employment agency was seen not only as an instrument of flexibility in large companies but also, in the context of the labor market, as a whole.

V.1.   Internal regulations on work through a temporary employment agency

The current Labor Code regulates for the first time work through a temporary employment agency[64]. According to art. 88, it means the work of a temporary employee who has signed a temporary contract with a temporary employment agency and works temporarily under the supervision and direction of the user. According to art. 88 para. 5 of the Labor Code temporary work assignment means the period during which the temporary employee is available to the user to work temporarily under their supervision and leadership to execute a specific temporary task.

Work through a temporary employment agency involves delivery of legal relationships between three distinct persons[65]:

- Temporary employee - the person assigned to an employer, that is, a temporary employment agency, and made available to a user during necessary to perform specific tasks and temporary;

- Temporary employment agency - legal person authorized by the Ministry of Labor, Family and Social Protection, which

---

[64] To analyze this type of employment contract, see I.T.Ştefănescu, Ş. Beligrădeanu, Prezentare de ansamblu şi observaţii critice asupra noului Cod al muncii, in „Dreptul" no. 4/2003, p. 5; D. Ţop, Codul muncii comentat, Impact Publishing House, Târgovişte, 2003; V. Zanfir, Codul muncii comentat, Tribuna Economică, Bucureşti, 2004; Al. Athanasiu, L. Dima, Dreptul muncii, All Beck Publishing House, Bucureşti, 2005, p. 72-76; Al. Ţiclea, Tratat de dreptul muncii, Rosetti Publishing House, Bucureşti, 2006, p. 522-529; N. Voiculescu, Dreptul muncii. Reglementări interne şi comunitare, Wolters Kluwer Publishing House, Bucureşti, 2007; I.T. Ştefănescu, Tratat de dreptul muncii, Wolters Kluwer Publishing House, Bucureşti, 2007, p. 415-421
[65] Al. Athanasiu, L. Luminiţa, Dreptul muncii, All Beck Publishing House, Bucureşti, 2005, p. 273

provides for the user available qualified and/or unqualified staff, which is hired and paid to do so;

- The user - the person or entity to which the temporary employment agency shall provide a temporary employee to perform certain specific and temporary tasks.

The employment contract is concluded between the temporary employment agency and temporary employee (Labor Code Section 94). Between a temporary employment agency and the user a provision contract is concluded (Art. 91 para. 1).

The regulation in the Labor Code regarding temporary employment agency is in compliance with Directive 2008/104/EC of the European Parliament and of the Council of 19 November 2008 on temporary agency work[66].

Between the temporary employment agency and the temporary employee an employment contract of limited duration is concluded for a mission. Assignments shall be for a term of not less than 24 months. The mission's duration may be extended for successive periods, which, added to the initial period should not result in exceeding a period of 36 months. The temporary employment contract must contain details concerning the conditions under which the employee will perform his mission, the mission, identity and location of

the user, amount and remuneration arrangements provided by the temporary employee.

Two diametrically opposed opinions have been expressed in the legal literature on the form of the contract of employment between a temporary employment agency and a tem-

---

[66] Published in Official Journal of European Union, Series L 327, December 5, 2008

porary employee. Thus, it was argued[67] that the written form is a condition of *ad validitatem* of the temporary work contract, due to the fact that the contract 'is an auxiliary document that can only be concluded as based on the existence of an availability agreement contract', which is necessarily concluded in writing as a condition of ad validity. In this case, from applying the *accesorium sequitur* principle, the written form of temporary employment contract would also be ad validity prerequisite.

The temporary employment contract may set a probationary period in accordance with art. 97 of the Labor Code, at the request of the user company. The contract may last between two and thirty working days, depending on the total duration of temporary contracts and the duties performed by the temporary employee.

The temporary employee is entitled to a salary for each task and the salary level negotiated directly with the temporary employment agency, cannot be lower than the gross minimum guaranteed payment. To ensure receipt of wages by the temporary employee, the Labor Code, art. 96 para. 5 provides that users pay for these rights if the temporary employment agency is more than 15 days overdue with fulfilling the requirement. After fulfilling this obligation, the user company is subrogated to the rights of the temporary employee against the temporary employment agency.

The contract of employment concluded between a temporary employment agency and a temporary employee is usually terminated on the expiry date of the mission or missions

---

[67] V. Popa, O. Pană, Dreptul muncii comparat, Lumina Lex Publishing House, București, 2003, p. 103; Al. Ambrozie, St. Naubauer, Organizarea muncii prin agent de muncă temporară conform noului Cod al muncii, in „Revista română de dreptul muncii" nr. 1/2003, p. 95-96; Al. Țiclea, Tratat de dreptul muncii, Rosetti Publishing House, București, 2006

for which it was concluded. However, the temporary employment agency, like any other employer, may dismiss the
temporary employee, but only as provided by law, as in the
case of the other employees.

Between the temporary employee and the user no contract is
concluded. Legal relations between them are established by
the law and are governed by the principle of non-
discrimination[68], temporary employees having access to all
the services and facilities provided by the user, in the same
conditions as the other employees (Art. 92 para. 1). The user
is responsible for ensuring working conditions to the temporary employee. Also, the provisions of the collective labor
contract concluded at the user's level shall be applied with
no discrimination to both temporary employees and the user's own employees. At the end of the mission, the temporary
employee user may conclude an individual contract of employment with the user.

V.2.   EU regulations on work through a temporary
employment agency

In countries of the former European Economic Community,
the activity of intermediation on the labor market, as well as
recruitment and temporarily assigning employees to other
companies in order to meet short term labor needs were, for
a long time, activities generally prohibited because, legally,
it was considered that they were using practices that were
against the fundamental rights of workers.

---

[68] Al. Athanasiu, L. Dima, Dreptul muncii, All Beck Publishing House, Bucureşti, 2003,
p. 103; Al. Ambrozie, St. Naubauer, Organizarea muncii prin agent de muncă
temporară conform noului Cod al muncii, in „Revista română de dreptul muncii" no.
1/2003, p. 95-96; Al. Ţiclea, Tratat de dreptul muncii, Rosetti Publishing House,
Bucureşti, 2005, p. 277

However, by the late sixties, many countries in the European Economic Community, although having already ratified Convention 96/1949 of the International Labor on private work placement agencies, had also regulated the temporary employment agency business. It was understood that this activity, when conducted in a controlled way, did not only cause damage, but had also positive effects. It allowed channeling much of the job supply, which, because of the specialization and of the need to get an immediate response could not be adequately addressed by the employment services of traditional public employment.

In this regard, it is considered that the weak point is not represented by the activity of the temporary employment agency, but by its lack of regulation and control of the labor market emergence of illegal subjects who did not provide even the most basic guarantees of labor rights and social protection for employees. In terms of institutions and Community law, the free movement of workers and the principle of free competition, the emergence of temporary employment agencies appear to be legitimate.

The Court of Justice has determined that public employment offices to which the law of a Member State assigns the management of general economic interest services should be subject to the rules on competition under Art. 90 para. 2 of the Treaty, as long as it is demonstrated that the application is incompatible with performing their duties[69]. Later, the Court of Justice decided to relate the temporary employment agencies to the notion of freedom to provide services[70].

---

[69] Judgment of the European Court of Justice, 30 April 1974, C-155/73, Case Sacchi, para.15
[70] Judgment of the European Court of Justice, 17 December 1981, C-279/80, Case Webb

The community court established[71] that competition law should consider a 'firm' any entity, public or private, engaged in an economic activity, regardless of the legal status and of the financing of that entity. Also, the activity aimed at placing workforce is an economic activity that has not always been and should not to be exercised by public enterprises. Thus, when those offices do not meet conditions to fulfill the demand that exists in the labor market, for all types of activities, attributing the state exclusive rights to exploit the service would involve an abuse of its dominant position. This is contrary to the rules of the Treaty governing competition, for service provision is limited to the detriment of users. Thus, national laws which prohibit any activity of mediation or interposition between labor supply and demand, activity which is exercised by public employment offices, attempt at art. 86 and Art. 90 para. 1 of the Treaty[72].

This creates responsibility of the Member State which favors it, keeping that legislation, when the abusive behavior may affect trade between Member States, without the need for the trade damage to have actually occurred. In fact, it is sufficient to have a potentially abusive situation[73].

The Directive covers the principle of equal treatment under which assigned employees must be treated, during the mission, at least as favorable as the comparable employee of the user firm. The equal treatment refers to the essential conditions of work and employment, including those which are

---

[71] Judgment of the European Court of Justice, 11 December 1997, C-55/96, Case Job Centre Coop, para. 21, 22, 31, 32, 35
[72] Judgment of the European Court of Justice, 11 December, 1997, C55/96, Case Job Centre Coop, para. 35 and 38
[73] Judgment of the European Court of Justice, 11 December, 1997, C55/96, Case Job Centre Coop, para. 36

dependent on a specific seniority in the job, except when there are objective reasons that justify a different treatment.

When there is no comparable employee in a user firm, the comparison will be made taking into account a comparable employee in the applicable collective agreement. If the user firm has no collective agreement applicable, then the reporting element will be found in the collective agreement applicable to the temporary employment agency. In the absence of an applicable collective labor agreement, national law and practice shall be referred to.

To avoid precarious work in the case of a temporary employee, there is an obligation to inform the assigned employees on existing vacancies in the user firm in order to facilitate their employment. In addition, it is proposed to oblige Member States to take measures for considering invalid the clauses prohibiting the conclusion of an individual employment contract between a user firm and a temporary employee, after completing the mission.

In regulating access to training, the Directive attaches great munificence in action to Member States so that, either in accordance with national traditions and practice, with collective bargaining, or by taking necessary measures, they would improve access to training employees assigned by the temporary employment agent to the user firm.

In terms of collective representation, the Directive requires that assigned employees be taken into account by the temporary employment agent in order to determine the threshold for constituting collective employee representation bodies.

Finally, the Directive requires that the user firm shall inform the legal representatives of employees on the use of temporary assignment of employees within the company, when the information on the employment situation is transmitted to the respective representatives.

VI.   The on-the-job apprenticeship contract

VI.1.   The internal regulation of the on-the-job apprenticeship contract

In the Romanian law, the contract of apprenticeship is regulated by the Labor Code, Law no. 279/2005[74] on the on-the-job apprenticeship and the implementation rules of this legal provision approved by Government Ordinance no. 129/2000 on adult professional training[75].

The apprenticeship contract is an individual employment contract of a particular type, under which a person, called an apprentice, undertakes to prepare professionally and work for and under the authority of a legal or natural person named employor, who undertakes to ensure payment of wages and all the conditions necessary for the professional training[76].

The apprenticeship contract must expressly stipulate certain additional clauses to the general clauses of the classic individual labor contract content, namely:

- The qualification, or skills that the apprentice must acquire;

- The name of his master apprenticeship and his qualification;

- The location of the professional training activity;

- The program distribution of practical and theoretical training, as appropriate;

- The time required to obtain qualifications or skills;

---

[74] Republished in Official Gazette of Romania, Part I, no. 498, August 7, 2013
[75] Republished in Official Gazette of Romania, Part I, no. 110, February 13, 2014
[76] Al. Athansiu, L. Dima, Dreptul muncii, All Beck Publishing House, București, 2005, p. 238

- Benefits in kind provided for the apprentice.

The apprentice is applied all provisions relating to the status of an employee to the extent that they are not contrary to the ones specific to the status of the apprentice. Under the provisions of art. Article 8. 2 of Law no. 279/2005 on the on-the-job apprenticeship, the employer may require the apprentice to include in the contract the obligation to remain in the firm for a certain period of time after being professionally trained. Otherwise, the apprentice undertakes to reimburse the expenditure incurred by the employer with his training.

The apprenticeship contract is concluded on a fixed term of between six months and three years and the apprentice benefits from the entire rights of other employees if they do not contradict his status.

Essentially, the apprenticeship contract is a contract of employment, of a particular type, concluded and executed under specific conditions. Thus, the parties that may enter into an apprenticeship contract must meet certain conditions, namely:

a. According to art. 5 of Law no. 279/2005 any person over the age of 16 but not more than 25 years can be classified as an apprentice, as long as they do not have a qualification for the occupation for which the on-the-job apprenticeship is organized. Individuals aged 15 to 16 years may also enter an apprenticeship contract if three cumulative conditions are fulfilled, namely:

- There is written consent of parents or legal guardians;

- Activities to be undertaken are appropriate to the physical development, skills and knowledge of the child;

- The apprenticeship contract shall not endanger the health, development and training of the child.

b. According to art. 6 of Law no. 279/2005, only legal entities and natural persons authorized by the Ministry of Labor, Family and Equal Opportunities may conclude a contract of apprenticeship as employers. Authorized individuals and family businesses can act as employers, notwithstanding the provisions of Government Emergency Ordinance no. 44/2008 that limit the capacity for other types of contracts.

The apprenticeship contract is concluded in a written form in Romanian and recorded by the Labor Inspectorate in whose jurisdiction the employer operates. In addition, the employer is required to register the contract of apprenticeship in the general register of employees compiled electronically.

A special feature of the contract of apprenticeship is the quality needed by the foreman under whose guidance the apprentice is formed. Thus, the foreman must be hired by the employer and approved for this purpose by the Ministry of Labor, Family and Equal Opportunities. He is responsible for coordinating the activities of the apprentice.

Considering these aspects, the legislature explained the legal nature of the contract of apprenticeship, that is, the contract was qualified as a particular type of work contract, with a complex object. The object is not represented only by the labor supply and by paying the salary, but also by the training of apprentice in a particular job, an element that is crucial for this type of contract[77].

---

[77] Al. Ţiclea, Tratat de dreptul muncii, Rosetti Publishing House, Bucureşti, 2006, p. 249

In the literature[78] it was stated that this type of individual employment contract has the general features of this legal act, as well as specific features. Thus, the contract of apprenticeship is, on the one hand, a contract called bilateral synallagmatic, commutative, onerous, *intuitu personae*, with sequential execution, characterized by the relationship of subordination between apprentice and employer, and, on the other hand, is characterized by the following:

- It is part of the professional training, according to art. 193 letter d) of the Labor Code;

- It is a fixed-term contract;

- A legal individual work relationship is based on it;

- The cause of the contract is unique, incorporating both the training of apprentices and their work and salary.

In conclusion, as stated in the doctrine[79], 'the main factor of qualifying the contract of apprenticeship as an employment contract of a particular type is the fact that – along with the objective of training - providing employment and salary benefits are characteristics of this type of contract'.

Currently, in the country, according to data published by Labor inspection, there registered apprenticeship contracts at work, which means that employers are less interested in this way of training.

VI.2.   Community legislation for on-the-job apprenticeship

[78] See I.T. Ştefănescu, Tratat de dreptul muncii, Wolters Kluwer Publishing House, Bucureşti, 2007, p. 427
[79] I.T. Ştefănescu, Tratat de dreptul muncii, Wolters Kluwer Publishing House, Bucureşti, 2007, p. 429

contracts

At Community level there are currently no legal regulations of the contract of apprenticeship. Community institutions are interested in this type of employment contract. Thus, the Council adopted the Resolution of the 18th of December 1979 on alternating formation of youth[80], and, on the 20th of December 1996, Conclusions on the ongoing apprenticeship strategy[81]. These documents established a set of principles for this type of work relationship, namely[82]:

a. The actions performed must respect the balance between personal, cultural and civic interests and the concerns about the economy and jobs;

b. Apprenticeship should be based on the possibility to choose from a wide range, allowing apprentices to progress in their education, according to their interests and their social, cultural and economic needs;

c. Initial education and training are fundamental to apprenticeship;

d. Apprenticeship should be aimed at developing individual capacities, at strengthening the ability of young people to obtain a job, at promoting an optimal use of resources and of human talent, eliminating social exclusion;

e. Apprenticeship enables apprentices to seek to develop responsibility for their own education and training;

f. Individuals, institutions, businesses, local governments, social partners, and society generally must create the conditions necessary to establish a positive attitude towards apprenticeship.

---

[80] Published in Official Journal of European Union, Series C1, January 3, 1980
[81] Published in Official Journal of European Union, Series C7, January 10, 1997
[82] See O. Ţinca, Contractul de ucenicie în dreptul comparat, in „Revista română de dreptul muncii" no. 2/2003, p. 51 – 59

It should be noted, however, that the apprentices still benefit from the protection of Community law by Directive 94/33/EC of 22 June 2004 on the protection of young people at work[83], whose aims fall within the following coordinates:

- Member States shall take the necessary measures to prohibit child labor. They will ensure that minimum employment age is not lower than the age at which compulsory schooling under national law is completed and, in any case, not lower than 15 years;

- Member States shall ensure that the work of adolescents is strictly regulated and protected in accordance with the terms of the Directive;

- Member States shall ensure that employers guarantee that young people's working conditions are appropriate to their age[84].

It should be noted that the International Labor Organization has developed two recommendations which contain references to on-the-job apprenticeship, namely, Recommendation no. 57/1939 and Recommendation no. 60/1939. As mentioned in the literature[85], these international documents define apprenticeship as any system where the employer is contractually obliged to hire a young man whom he teaches or whom he makes methodically learn a trade within a fixed period. Thus, the person concerned is obliged to perform work in the service of the employer.

The analysis of international documents, compared with the national ones referring to apprenticeship on the job, it is noted that, in general, the national legislature considered

---

[83] Published in Official of European Union, Series L 216, August 20, 1994
[84] See A. Popescu, Dreptul internaţional al muncii, C.H. Beck Publishing House, Bucureşti, 2006, p. 536
[85] See I.T. Ştefănescu, Tratat de dreptul muncii, Wolters Kluwer Publishing House, Bucureşti, 2007, p. 429

international rules, but, as stated in the doctrine, there are some gaps that could be filled by subsequent amendments to the legislation. Thus, in the literature, proposals *de lege ferenda* were made[86] in this regard, proposals considered appropriate, and exposed briefly below:

- Young people aged at least 15 years could conclude a contract of apprenticeship on the job, even if they have completed only their primary education. Under the current law, in order to conclude a contract of apprenticeship, the young person must be a graduate of 10 year-compulsory education;

- The maximum age of 25 years for an apprentice should be overcome, in the case of the disabled or when the apprentice had completed an apprenticeship contract which was terminated for non-attributable reasons , before the deadline;

Establishing the territorial labor inspoctorato right to suspend the contract of apprenticeship on the job in case of a risk of an occupational disease or of physical or mental injury of the apprentice. During the suspension, however, the employer must pay the apprentice a compensatory allowance. If the risks that led to the suspension of the contract of apprenticeship are not eliminated, the contract should be terminated and the employer is obliged to compensate the apprentice.

- The possibility to extend the contract in the case of failure of the apprentice in the final professional evaluation;

- Regulating specific conditions of termination of the apprenticeship contract, in order to enhance the protection

---

[86] I.T. Ştefănescu, Tratat de dreptul muncii, Wolters Kluwer Publishing House, Bucureşti, 2007, p. 439-440

of the apprentice, by establishing territorial labor inspectorate notice requirement for the dismissal of the apprentice.

Title VI
Individual Labour Disputes And Work Jurisdiction

According to art. 231 of the Labour Code, labour conflicts are disputes between employees and employers regarding their interests in the economic, social or professional fields or referring to rights arising from employment relationships.

It is essential that any individual labour dispute involves the existence of a legal relationship, based on an individual or collective labour contract, on which a disagreement between the employee and the employer or between the social partners is recorded at a certain time.

Law no. 62/2011 regarding social dialogue classifies labour disputes as follows:

-*Individual labour disputes*

-*Collective labour disputes*

I.   Individual labour disputes

Individual labour conflicts are defined as labour disputes that refer to the exercise of rights and fulfillment of obligations arising from laws or other regulations , as well as from collective or individual employment contracts, and also from the law or other regulations (art. 1 letter p) of Law no. 62/2011).

Another category of individual labour conflicts are disputes on the conclusion, execution modification, suspension and termination of individual employment contracts.

This can trigger individual conflicts for:

- Disciplinary sanctions;

- Dismissal;

- Unilateral changes in contract terms;

- Unpaid wages;

- Ascertainment of individual employment contracts that are void.

There are also individual labour disputes those conflicts connected with the execution and termination of collective agreement or its nullity, being excluded from this category conflicts in connection with the conclusion of collective agreements.

Individual labour disputes are settled only by judicial process, whereas collective labour conflicts have a special procedure for settlement, including conciliation, mediation and arbitration.

II.   Labour jurisdiction

Labour jurisdiction covers the settlement of labour disputes on the conclusion, performance, amendment, suspension and termination of individual employment contracts or, where applicable, collective labour contracts provided by the Labour Code. Labour jurisdiction also deals with requests regarding the application of legal relations between social partners established under the Labour Code.

II.1. The panel of judges

The panel that aims at resolving court cases involving labour disputes consists of one judge and two judicial assistants. For resolving the appeal there is a panel that consists of two judges.

Assistants who settle causes of labour disputes in the first instance are part of the judicial advisory, participating in deliberations and signing judgments. Their opinion is recorded in the judgment and dissenting opinion is justified. Judicial assistants are appointed by the Justice Minister at the proposal of the Economic and Social Council for a period of five years.

II.2. Material and territorial competence of the courts

The court usually resolves individual labour disputes as a court of first instance.

Other courts (courts of appeal and the High Court of Cassation and Justice) are competent to adjudicate in such disputes only when exercising judicial review, therefore, examining appeals within the limits and under the conditions provided by law.

a) **Material competence**

The court has unlimited jurisdiction with regard to the settlement of conflicts of rights, addressing the following:

- Labour disputes referring to claims on money, regardless of the   amount;

- Appeals against termination of the labour contract and labour disputes on work reintegration, including that of managers designated by superior bodies, as well as of directors, general managers and disputes related to the conclusion and execution of this contract ;

- Appeals against redeployment of staff, made during downsizing;

- Appeals against unilateral changes to wages set according to statutory provisions;

- Complaints against disciplinary sanctions;

- Action for annulment of payment commitments;

- Disputes in connection with the execution, suspension and termination of the collective employment contracts;

b)   Territorial jurisdiction

The competent court designated to resolve conflicts of rights is the one in whose jurisdiction the applicant resides.

II.3.   Deadlines for court referral

Applications for settlement of individual labour disputes must be made by those whose rights were violated in compliance with deadlines set by law. Non-compliance with these deadlines causes rejection of the request by the competent court as being late filed.

Thus, the applications for resolving a work conflict can be formulated according to the Labour Code:

- Within 30 calendar days from the date the unilateral decision of the employer on the conclusion , performance, amendment , suspension or termination of the individual employment contract was communicated;

 - Within 30 calendar days from the date of notification of the disciplinary sanction;

 - Within 3 years from the establishment of the right of action, if the subject of the individual labour conflict consists in the payment of outstanding wages or damages to the employee, as well as in the case of employee liability towards employers;

- On the whole duration of the contract, if the establishment of the nullity of an individual contract or collective bargaining agreement is requested; ;

- Within 6 months from the date when the right of action was established, in case of non-execution of collective bargaining agreement or clauses thereof ;

- In all other cases, the term is 3 years from the date when the right was established.

According to art. 211 of Law no. 62/2011, applications may be made by those whose rights have been violated as follows:

a) unilateral measures of enforcement, modification, suspension or termination of the individual employment contract, including commitments to pay certain sums of money, may be appealed within 45 calendar days of the date on which the party concerned became aware of the measure ordered;

b) the ascertainment of the nullity of an individual employment contract may be requested by the parties throughout the period in which the contract applies;

c) paying compensation for the damage caused and restitution of amounts which formed the subject of undue payment may be required within 3 years from the date of damage.

II.4.   Appeal

Court of first instance decisions are under appeal only. The deadline for the appeal is 10 days from the notification of the judgment. Lack of any appeal and failure to fulfill any act of legal proceedings within the deadline attract forfeiture, unless the law provides otherwise or when there is evidence provided by the party that it was prevented by circumstances beyond their will.

II.5.   Stamp duty

All applications for settlement of labor disputes are exempt from judicial stamp and stamp duty.

Part 2
German Labour Law

Foreword

German law is part of a European legal system which follows the tradition of Roman law. All important legal issues are covered by extensive legislation in the form of statutes, codes and regulations.

Whereas German civil law is rooted in the Roman 'ius com-mune,' the history and the development of labour law started in the industrialization era of the 19th century. Germany was the first country – after England – to pass labour laws.

Regulations concerning child labour were established in Prussia in 1839, whereby the employment of children under 9 years of age was prohibited, and children under the age of 16 were only allowed to work ten hours a day.

In 1863 the German Workers Association was founded, and the Industrial Code, which was established in 1869, was the next step towards the creation of a legal system to protect workers. From 1878 onwards, Bismarck's government passed a series of laws intended to protect the working class, such as the Health Insurance Act, Accident and Disablement Insurance and Provisions for Old Age, all of which were part of the beginnings of social security.

Since the Weimar Republic, after the end of World War I, protection against unfair dismissal has been a key element of German labour law. This was laid down in Section 84 of the Works Councils Act of 1920. In 1926 a special labour court jurisdiction was established by the Labour Courts Act and all disputes concerning labour law were decided by the labour courts and no longer by the ordinary civil courts.

All trade unions and employers` associations were dissolved during the National Socialist era, and working life was regulated by the state. The fundamental features of the Weimar regulations concerning protection against unfair dismissals were retained in Section 56 of the National Labour Act of 1934.

After the end of World War II, the newly established Federal Republic drew up the German Constitution (Grundgesetz – GG) and labour laws were developed further. The re-founded States (Länder) established the Acts on the Protection against Unfair Dismissals,which mainly reverted to the model of the Weimar Republic.

There is no general code for labour law in Germany. Employment law is based on the Constitution and various statutes, ordinances and legal provisions. It develops from rulings of the Labour Courts, especially those of the German Federal Labour Court. Employment law is a complex issue, and is not without inconsistencies.

This textbook is a concise guide of the basics of labour law and the individual employment relationship between employers and employees. It is intended for readers who are looking for a short overview and reliable information on the fundamentals of German Labour Law.

Schrobenhausen – 2014

Ilona Zenker

Title I
General Considration of the Individual Emplyment Contract

Chapter 1

I.   In General

I.1.   Conditions of an Individual Employment Contract

The individual employment contract is neither legally defined nor legally standardized. The employment contract was developed out of the service contract, codified in the German Civil Code (Bürgerliches Gesetzbuch – BGB).

This is the reason why up to the present day all legal regulations of the service contract in the German Civil Code (BGB) still apply to the individual employment contract. According to Section 611 of the German Civil Code (BGB), a service contract is in force whenever the provision of any services is owed by one party of the contracting parties. However, it must be pointed out that the service contract is different from the individual employment contract because of the greater mutual rights and duties of the parties. The reason for this is a personal dependence of the employee on the employer, concerning working time, the working place and the kind of work required of the employee.

The guiding principle of German labour law is freedom of contract, which means that the employer is free to choose with whom he wants to conclude an employment contract.

The employment contract arises from two corresponding declarations of intent by the two contracting parties, without any formal requirements. The principle of freedom of contract implicates that no special formalities are required and the contract can even be concluded by an oral statement. According to the Act of Documentation of Employment Conditions (Nachweisgesetz – NachwG), the employee has the right to claim a written documentation of the essential contents of the employment contract.

But that does not mean that the observance of the written form is required to conclude a valid labour contract. The legal restrictions on freedom of contract will be explained later.

I.2.   Distinctions and other Types of Contract

The service contract must be distinguished from several other kinds of contracts.

The service contract and hence the individual employment contract is different from an "assignment" or "order" as stated in Section 662 BGB, which is free of charge. The employment contract must also be distinguished from the "contract of work and services" as stated in Section 631 of the German Civil Code (BGB), because the employee is not pledged to succeed, but only to work.

I.3.   Contract Parties

a.   Employees

In German Labour Law there is no statutory provision defining the notion of "employee". According to Section 84 of the Commercial Code (Handelsgesetzbuch – HGB), there is only a legal definition of the term "self-employed". A self-employed person is free to organise her / his work and to determine her / his working time.

There are different factors that indicate the status of an employee. An employee is a person who is obliged to work for an employer because of a private contract, and who is in a relationship of personal subordination. This subordination is a combination of personal subordination and economic dependence. The employee is integrated into the employer`s organisation, has to follow the directives of the employer and carries no economic risks.

The distinction between manual workers, the so called "blue-collar workers", who mainly work with their hands and do manual labour and the so-called "white-collar workers", who are employees mainly involved in brainwork, has historical origins. The distinguishing features of these two groups were laid down in the occupational classification of Section 133 paragraph 2 of the old version of the Social Security Code (Sozialgesetzbuch - SGB), which was in effect until the beginning of 2005.

The white-collar workers were better paid, had longer periods of notice and were covered by a special statutory pension system. With the advance of technological progress this classification disappeared, as it was incompatible with the principle of equal treatment (Article 3 of the German Constitution – Grundgesetz GG). Although the notion of manual workers and employees can still be found in legal texts, although the two groups are no longer treated differently.

As stated above, the factors indicating the status of an employee are numerous. We are therefore going to define the notion of the employee by describing groups of working people who are not defined as employees in terms of German labour law.

Guide for Romanian and German Labour Law
Basics of the Employment Relationship

> **Employee-like Persons**

Employee-like persons are neither "self-employed" nor employees as described above. "Employee-like" persons are not
covered by labour law as a whole, but only by some specific
sections. The fundamental distinction between them is the
"economic and personal dependence on the one group and
the "independence" of the other group.

Employee-like persons are not integrated into the operational
labour organisation of the employer, can freely determine
their actions and their working time, have to do most of their
duties themselves and perform their work - for one or more
employer - for more than half of their average income, which
is paid by one employer. For these reasons employee-like
persons are not dependent on an employer in the same way
or to the same extent as ordinary, regular employees. Therefore employee-like persons are not protected from dismissal,
for example, but they can sue either in labour or industrial
courts.

"Commercial agents", who are prohibited by contract to
work for other companies, also belong in this category. Most
of the mutual duties of the parties are mainly written down in
the Commercial Code (Handelsgesetzbuch – HGB).

In the same way, "homeworkers" also belong to employee-
like persons, because they work either alone or with help of
family members at a place of their own choosing, and can
dispose of their working time freely. Their rights are specified
in the Act of Homework (Heimarbeitergesetz – HAG)

> **Executive Staff**

Members of the executive staff have an exceptional position.
Due to their function and their authority to take decisions

they should be compared to employers rather than to employees.

The legal definition of the notion "Executive Staff" is not uniform and depends on the legal context in which it is used.

The Act on Dismissal Protection (Kündigungsschutzgesetz - KSchG) defines these employees - in a different way from the Works Constitution Act (Betriebsverfassungsgesetz - BetrVG) – according to their function in the company, the legal problems connected to their position and the decisions, that they make which affect other employees of the company.

The Act of Working Time (Arbeitszeitgesetz – ArbZG) and the Works Constitution Act (Betriebsverfassungsgesetz – BetrVG) do not apply to the executive staff. The Act on Dismissal Protection (Kündigungsschutzgesetz – KSchG) only partly covers members of the executive staff. They are treated as a separate group of employees, and are not fully protected by law in the same way as regular employees.

> **Freelancers**

Freelancers are classified as self-employed and independent contractors. They are personally independent, create their own working conditions, are not bound to the instructions of an employer, can determine their manner and the time in which they work, and are paid according to their actual working performance. This mode of employment is mainly used in newspaper enterprises and in the food service industry. Free collaborators have no legal protection in case of illness and are not entitled to paid vacation.

This legal concept made it possible for employers to bypass the legal cancellation protection for their employees, and to avoid paying social insurance for them. The jurisdiction of the

German Federal Court of Labour decided that the parties of a contract cannot define the classification of their relationship by mutual agreement in order to escape the protection of labour law and social insurance.

The assessment of the relationship determines whether the contract is classified as a labour contract or a service contract of an independent contractor and depends on the outward appearance of the relationship and not on the heading or wording of the mutual agreement. The degree of personal subordination and the economic dependency of the freelancer will finally decide on the legal status.

> **Civil Servants**

The centrepiece of the employer-employee relationship is the individual labour contract, which is a private contract according to Section 611 of the German Civil Code (Bürgerliches Gesetzbuch – BGB). Therefore career public servants are therefore excluded from the labour law, because their relationship to the state is not based on a private contract, but on civil service law (Beamtenrecht), which is part of public law. Their rights and duties are established by acts of the Federal Republic, and disputes are settled by administrative courts instead of labour courts.

According to Article 33 paragraph V of the German Constitution (Grundgesetz – GG), judges and soldiers are not defined as employees either, because their public relationship to their employer – the state – is based on an administrative act and not on a contract.

On the other hand, ordinary employees who are not civil servants but work in the public sector are covered by labour law, because their contractual relationship is based on a private individual labour contract.

b.   Employers

The employer as the counterpart and contract partner of the employee can either be a natural or individual person, or a legal person in form of a corporate body. At all events the employer has to have at least one employee.[87]

If a corporate body like, for example, a public limited company, is in the position of an employer, the legal person cannot exercise authority or issue directives, because the entity is not capable of acting. The official organ acts for the juristic person and the operating manger must always be a natural person, who then acts as an employer.

II.   Theories about the scources of the individual employment relationship.

II.1.   Integration Theory

In the past, the "theory of integration" laid down that the individual employment contract was not established by the conclusion of the labour contract alone, but rather by the integration of the employee into the organisation of the employer's company. The employer-employee relationship thus consisted of two elements, and the employment contract was considered to be the first step only, giving the employee the right to be engaged and integrated by the employer. The second step was fulfilled when the employee actually started working[88]. This legal structure was very complicated and proved to be insufficient, as the employer could refuse to in-

---

[87]   BGH NJW 1981,1270
[88]   Nikisch, Arbeitsrecht, 1. Auflage 1951, Seite 81

tegrate the employee into his enterprise and then deny him his wages.

II.2. Contractual Theory

The contractual theory stipulates that the individual employment contract is established by the conclusion of the contract, and that the ensuing start of employment merely puts this into effect.[89]

According to the German Federal Labour Court, the contractual theory now has undisputed priority.[90].

Chapter II

Sources of German Labour Law and the Employment Relationship

I.   Law of Nations / International Law / Law of European Union

I.1.   Law of Nations

The employee-employer relationship is no longer subject to national industrial law alone, but to a mixture between supranational and national law. Only the supranational law, guaranteed by Art 24 and Art 25 of the German Constitution (Grundgesetz – GG), is valid beyond national boundaries and forms the basis of intergovernmental agreements protecting the interests of employees.

a.   International Labour Organisation (IAO)

Initially, the duty of the International Labour Organisation (IAO) – an independent specialized agency of the UNO in

---

[89] BAG NZA 1998,752
[90] BAG NZA 2002,1177

Geneva – was to create uniform occupational safety measures within different countries. So far, the Federal Republic of
Germany has ratified only 82 of the 188 conventions of the International Labour Organisation (IAO), and the degree of direct legal influence these IAO agreements have on the relationship between employees, employers and trade unions, is
still a matter of dispute.

**b.   European Convention of Human Rights and
European Social Charter**

In contrast to the 1950 European Convention of Human
Rights, which is valid in German federal law, the question of
whether the agreements of the European Social Charter are
legally binding in matters between German employees and
German employers, is still a subject of controversy.

I.2.   International Law

A distinction must be made between the supranational law
mentioned above and the "international labour law" of Germany, as stated in the introductory Act to the German Civil
Code (EGBGB), which was replaced in 2008 by the clauses of
Rom I-VO and Rom II – VO.

The Clauses of this law refer especially to the case of German employees working in foreign countries, and foreign
employees working in Germany, and to the question of which
national labour law is applicable. According to Art 3 Rom I-
VO, the contract parties are basically free to determine
which national law comes into force. If such an agreement is
missing, as stated in Art 8 II Rom I-VO, the law of the country
in which the employee predominantly works comes into

force. This law is then conclusive for all aspects of the employment relationship.

I.3.   Law of the European Union

The Labour Law of the European Union comprises two parts – the primary and the secondary law. The former consists of the final form of the founding contract, ratified in Lisbon - 13.12.2007 – and its amendments and alterations, while the latter incorporates all the by-laws and regulations. The secondary law is mandatory and replaces contrary national law.

The relationship between the Labour Law of the European Union and the German Labour Law is not clear in all details. Some decisions of the European Court received widespread attention, e.g. the compatibility of national law with the prohibition of sexual discrimination.

For the European Court of Justice (Europäischer Gerichtshof - EuGH) the law of the European Union is an independent system of laws. In the case of a conflict between the Law of the European Union and the German Labour Law, the Federal Constitutional Court (Bundesverfassungsgericht – BVerfGH) – the highest court of the Federal Republic of Germany - insists on its right to prove that the dispensation of justice accords with the fundamental rights of the German Constitution (Grundgesetz GG).

The European Court of Justice (ECJ) and the German Federal Constitutional Court (BVerfGH) finally agreed that European Law has priority, but that the regulations of the German national Labour Law are not invalid, only inapplicable.

Supranational law is still very much in the background in Germany, but time will bring increased awareness of the importance of international law.

II.   National Law

II.1.   Hierarchy of legal sources

The legal regulations used in German labour law are not summarized in one standardized code of law. Art 30 of the Unification Treaty of the Federal Republic of Germany includes a directive to create such a book of statutes. However all attempts have failed up to now, either because of resistance from divergent lobbies or because of the lack of clear directives from the legislator. In spite of the prospect of European integration, it is very unlikely that a comprehensive codification will be achieved.

Regulations concerning individual labour law, for example, are widely scattered in over 30 separate laws, including:

➢   Constitution (Grundgesetz – GG)

➢   Civil Code (Bürgerliches Gesetzbuch – BGB)

➢   Commercial Code (Handeslgesetzbuch – HGB)

➢   Dismissal Protection Act (Kündigungsschutzgesetz – KSchG)

➢   Act on Equal Treatment (Allgemeines Gleichbehandlungsgesetz – AGG)

➢   Act of Working Time (Arbeitszeitgesetz – ArbZG)

➢   Act of Commercial Temporary Work and Commercial Transfer of Employees (Arbeitnehmerüberlassungs-gesetz – AÜG)

➢   Act on the Improvement of Employment Opportunities (Beschäftigungsförderungsgesetz – BeschFG)

➢   Maternity Protection Act (Mutterschutzgesetz – MuSchG)

➢   Act on Parental Leave and Parental Time (Bundeselterngeld-und Elternzeitgesetz – BEEG)

Guide for Romanian and German Labour Law
Basics of the Employment Relationship

➢ Federal Vacations Act (Bundesurlaubsgesetz – BurlG)

➢ Act on Continued Payment of Remuneration on Holidays and in Case of Sickness (Entgeltfortzahlungsgesetz – EFZG)

➢ Trade Regulation Act (Gewerbeordnung – GewO)

➢ Act on Protection of Youth Employment (Jugendarbeitsschutzgesetz – JarbSchG)

➢ Act on Minimum Working Conditions (Gestz über Mindestarbeitsbedingungen – MindArbBedG)

➢ Act of the Documentation of Employment Conditions (Nachweisgesetz – NachwG)

➢ Act on Disabled Persons (Schwerbehindertengesetz – SchwbG)

➢ Act of Part-Time Work and Fixed-Term Employment (Teilzeit- und Befristungsgesetz – TzBfG)

➢ Act on Homework (Heimarbeitsgesetz – HAG)

➢ Social Code (Sozialgesetzbuch)

➢ Occupational Training Act (Berufsbildungsgesetz – BBiG)

The content of an individual labour contract is only valid if the conditions of the employer-employee relationship do not violate the law. Because of the huge number of individual laws, their interrelationship is of cardinal importance. This is the reason why the German legislator has created a mandatory ranking of all laws and provisions.

II.2. Constitution

At the top of the hierarchy of legal sources is the Constitution (Grundgesetz – GG), which plays a dominant role in individual labour law.

This is because of those constitutional rights which affect industrial law directly, like the right of personality (Art 1 and 2 GG), freedom of opinion and speech (Art 5 GG), freedom of conscience and belief (Art 5 GG), freedom to choose a career (Art 12 GG) and so on. The property right (Art 14 GG) and in particular the right to own the means of production are fundamental to the free market economy, and result in the superiority of employers. Labour law, which protects the rights of the employees, is based on the Social State Principle as specified in Art 20, 28 GG, and restricts the power of employers, regardless of their economic supremacy.

The working conditions of employees on the one hand and the employer's conditions of production on the other hand are inseparably linked. This is the reason why Art 9 section III GG consistently addresses the protection and improvement of both working and economic conditions. This combination of the interests of both parties is in step with national and global economic development, and must be adjusted to fit changing political and social aims. Thus Labour law will always remain in a state of evolution.

Legal problems not regulated by the legislator, or unclear legal or general terms, must be interpreted in the light of the basic rights of the Constitution, and it is in this way that the Constitution shapes the entire legal framework, affecting all other legal rulings indirectly. This clearly strengthens the power of the Federal Constitutional Court and judicial law, and influences the development of individual labour law.

II.3.   Ordinary Legislation

Because of the large numbers of legal provisions and acts – as described above – the level of protective legislation is comparatively high in Germany. Laws and ordinances affect the employment relationship. We have to distinguish between mandatory provisions on the one hand, which are not negotiable by the contract parties, and regulations on the other hand, which are alterable by mutual consent and are thus negotiable.

Mandatory regulations - like the Maternity Protection Act, Occupational Health and Safety Act, and Employment Protection Act – whose chief purpose is to protect the employees interests, are not alterable to the disadvantage of the employee. However, the contract parties are allowed to change the provisions in order to improve the conditions of the employees. In this case, the contract parties raise the level of protective rights above the legal standard. These are so called unilateral or partial mandatory provisions.

II.4.   Court Decisions

As mentioned above, the court decisions of the Federal Constitutional Court play a very important role in labour law. According to the Act on Court Procedure in Labour Law (Arbeitsgerichtsgesetz – ArbGG), the Federal Labour Court has the sole power to further expand labour law.

Parts of industrial law – like, for example, labour conflicts - are not fully regulated. The need for the specification and interpretation of general terms and rules, and the filling of legal gaps left open by the legislator, explain the importance of the German Federal Labour Court and justify its leading role.

Due to the technical, economical and social changes in the employment sector, the jurisdiction of the Federal Constitutional Court is frequently modified, and one can therefore safely say that nothing is more constant in this field than change. The employers and employees concerned have to struggle against highly unpredictable court decisions and legal uncertainty.

It must be stressed that "laws made by judges", or case law, is not an independant legal source. The binding force of the rulings of the German Federal Court must be qualified as "de facto".

The sentences that are pronounced depend on the specific facts and circumstances of each single case, and can be taken over as common or customary law in the course of time.

The question remains as to which extend the leading role of the Federal Labour Court still conforms to the principle of separation of power between the legislative and executive body, as laid down by the Constitution (Art 20.III. GG).

II.5.   Employment Contract

The function of the individual employment contract serves mainly to lay down the rights and duties of employees and employers, according to its contents. Although the employment contract is covered by, for example, protective laws, the individual employment contract, as stated in Section 611 of the German Civil Code (BGB), is the core of the employment relationship. It is basically entirely up to the parties involved to decide whether, with whom and under what conditions they conclude an employment contract. That is called freedom of contract.

This was taken to be an important improvement at the beginning of the 19th century. However, it later became evident that total freedom caused fierce competition amongst the employees, which led, in turn, to a worsening of the overall working condition. This unwanted and unfavourable development was, of course, only to the employers advantage, and resulted in restriction on the conclusion of employment contracts. The freedom of legal arrangement was further limited by several industrial safety regulations. Nevertheless, freedom of contract has survived as the basic idea and principle of individual labour law.

This is the unassailable rule concerning labour contracts with private employers. If an employee is instead applying for a job in the public sector, the employee cannot require the conclusion of a labour contract in general. The public employer has only the obligation to make a decision - using equitable discretion – whether to conclude a contract with that particular candidate or not.

II.6. Collective Agreements

The rights and duties of an employment contract can also be affected by collective agreements, known as union agreements. These are contracts between trade unions on the one hand, representing employees who are union members, and employer associations on the other hand, representing their members. Collective agreements are made up of two parts – the contractual and the normative section.

The former specifes the rights and duties of the contract parties, just like a private contract. The latter stipulates the regulations concerning the conclusion, content and termination of the employment relationship.

The clauses of a collective agreement only cover those members of a labour union whose employer is himself a member of an employer`s association, and who has finally signed a collective agreement. Then the union agreement is legally binding for these parties.

In certain circumstances the collective agreement can also have a direct effect on all individual employment relationships. This is the case when the collective agreement has been declared to be "generally binding" by the federal minister of employment, as laid down by Section 5 of the Act of Collective Agreement (Tarifvertragsgesetz – TVG). This declaration is a substitute for the absence of union membership on the part of an employee, or the missing membership to an employers association on the part of an employer.

Every collective agreement has a certain term, is limited to a particular geographical area and concerns a special branch in the world of work. If all these above conditions are fulfilled, the individual labour contract of an employee who is not a member of the trade union can thus be affected by such a union - or collective – agreement.

In some cases the union agreement may even fall below the minimum standards of working conditions stipulated by the legislator.

II.7. Company Agreements

Company agreements always cover the entire personnel of the company, whether they are union members or not. This work agreement is also called the "*law of the company*" and is a contract between the employer and the works council of the company. The clauses of a company agreement are as effective and as valid as a law, as stated in Section 77 paragraph IV of the Works Constitution Act (Betriebsverfassungsgesetz – BetrVG). Because of the principle of favourability, priority is given to those clauses of the individual employment contract which are more advantageous to the employee than the company agreement regulations.[91] The relationship between collective and company agreements as well the relationship between collective agreements and court decisions are subjects for constant and heated dispute.

II.8. General Conditions and Terms

Standardized or preformulated regulations used for a wide range of individual employment contracts, regardless of the special characteristics of a particular employment relationship, can be compared to general conditions and terms, or general business terms. If such general or preformulated terms are used in an individual working contract, they are only valid if they do not violate Section 305 of the Civil Code (Bürgerliches Gesetzbuch – BGB), or the ensuing terms which have replaced the law of general terms and conditions since 1.1.2002. According to Section 307, paragraph 1, sentence 2, of the German Civil Code (BGB), the principle of transparency demands from every user of such general terms that contract partners can identify their rights and duties clearly and unmistakably. In uncertain cases violation of the rules of transparency, or unreasonable discrimination, leads to invalidity of the used terms.

II.9. Custom

The regular repetition of certain behaviour – like the paying of an annual Christmas bonus, additional maternity benefit or vacation money – can become the subject of a claim by the employee, although there is no written agreement between the contract parties concerning these privileges or payments.

---

[91]   BAG NZA 1990,351

The fact of doing something repeatedly or permanently – mostly over a certain period of time - will be integrated into the working contract, if the employer intends to establish legal relations[92] and the employee can trust the employer to continue in this manner. Paying a certain bonus or premium three times running without any reservations obliges the employer to continue payment. These privileges granted voluntarily by the employer are called "Betriebliche Übung" and cannot be simply taken away.

The exact classification is controversial. According to the prevalent social contract theory, the permanent payment of a bonus is qualified as an offer from the employer, which is accepted by the employee indirectly by receiving and keeping the payment.

The privilege or the payment is then part of the employment contract and can be changed only by mutual consent or by a dismissal with the option of altered employment conditions.

II.10. Right to issue Instructions

The right to issue instructions gives the employer the right to specify the work expected of the employee. The employment contract usually only specifies the fundamentals of the employment relationship and not the details of the job performance. The vaguer the job description, the broader is the employer's right to issue instructions. The employment contract is not only the legal basis for this right, but also sets its limits, especially if the contract includes a detailed description of the sphere of activity.[93] The fact that an employee has been assigned to a certain job for a long period of time, may lead

---

[92]) BAG NZA 1998,423
[93]) BAG NZA 1990,561

him or her to claim for unaltered continuation, since these precise working conditions have become the content of the employment contract. This will/may limit the employer's right of instruction.

II.11.   Overview of the Ranking

The validity of the content of the employment relationship depends on a variety of factors, and because of the wide range of laws and regulations, the ranking and hierarchy of the legal sources and their relation to each other are decisive.

> **European Union Law**
>
> **German Constitution**
>
> **German Laws / mandatory**
>
> **Collective Agreements / mandatory**
>
> **Company Agreements / mandatory**
>
> **Individual Employment Contract**
>
> **General Terms and Conditions**
>
> **Custom**
>
> **Right to Issue Instructions**
>
> **German Law / dispensable**
>
> **Collective Agreements / dispensable**

Title II

General Conditions for the Conclusion of an Individual Employment Contract

Chapter I

Every employment agreement creates an employment relationship. The individual employment contract defines the specific working conditions for the employer and the employee, such as salary, working time or working place. Theterm "employment relationship" refers to the entire legal relationship between the contracting parties.

I.   Legal capacity

An employment contract is the result of two declarations of intent by the contracting parties – the offer and the acceptance of this offer as stated in Sections 145 and 147 German Civil Code (BGB – Bürgerliches Gesetzbuch). Full contractual capacity is an essential condition for a valid declaration of intent and hence for the valid conclusion of a contract. [94]

Persons who are legally incompetent – as laid down in Section 104 of the German Civil Code (BGB), or persons who have only limited legal capacity – as stated in Section 106 of the German Civil Code (BGB), - cannot normally conclude a valid contract or, as in this case, an individual employment contract.

---

[94] Palandt, Beck`sche Kurzkommentar, Bürgerliches Gesetzbuch, 2012, § 145, Rdr. 1 ff.

II.1.) Legal incapacity

According to Section 104 Nr. 1 BGB, all persons under the age of 7 are legally incompetent. [95]

Sections 104 Nr. 2 and Nr. 3 BGB have determined two other grounds for legal incompetence. Adults suffering from permanent mental disturbance, or persons officially placed under the control of a legal guardian on grounds of insanity, are legally incompetent.

All declarations of intent by such persons are null and void, according to Section 105 paragraph 1 of the German Civil Code (BGB). Not even the legal representative can confirm a statement of declared intent on the part of a legally incapable person.

In the case a legally capable person making a declaration of intent towards a legally incapable person, this statement becomes valid at the very moment the declaration reaches the legal representative of the legally incapable person, as laid down in Section 131 of the German Civil Code (BGB).

In accordance with Section 105 paragraph 2 of the German Civil Code (BGB), a declaration of intent is void if it is delivered to a person who is unconscious, or in a temporary state of mental disturbance, even if this person is basically legally capable.

II.2.) Limited legal capacity

Minors who are seven and over, but who have not yet reached their eighteenth birthday, are persons with limited legal capacity – as laid down in Section 106 of the German Civil Code (BGB).

---

[95] Palandt, Beck´scher Kurzkommentar, Bürgerliches Gesetzbuch, 71.Auflage, 2012, § 104 Rndr. 1 ff

Most legal transactions carried out by a person of limited legal capacity result in a provisionally ineffective contract. The transactions are only valid from the very beginning if the person with limited legal capacity has acted with the consent or permission of the legal representative, who is usually a parent of the minor. If this has been omitted, the legal transaction can be approved by the legal representative at a later date. In the meantime the legal action is only provisionally invalid.

There are some exceptions to this principle, as laid down in Sections 107 and 110 of the German Civil Code (BGB). If the declaration of intent is only of advantage to the minor, the legal action is valid right from the beginning, e.g. the acceptance of a gift which does not involve the personal commitment of the minor.

II.3. Underage Employees and Employers

Section 110 of the German Civil Code (BGB) is named "the pocket money section", and states that a contract concluded by a minor without the prior consent of his legal representative is valid from the beginning if the minor performs services in conformity with the contract and the money is given to him by the legal representative or by a third party who has been given the representative's consent for this purpose. [96]

Another exception is written down in Section 113 of the German Civil Code, which concerns under-age employees and their limited contractual capacity as minors. Minor employees can be qualified as fully legally competent if their legal representative – usually a parent - have authorized them to

---

[96] Münchener Kommentar zum Bürgerlichen Gesetzbuch mit Nebengesetzen, 5. Aufl., 2006-2010, § 110

conclude, fulfil or terminate an employment contract. The fully legal capacity of the minor employee is limited to affairs connected with the working place and its effects.[97]

This does not apply to vocational training contracts, because, according to the Vocational Training Act (Berufsausbildungsgesetz – BBiG), this kind of contract does not qualify as an employment contract.

An under-age employer - as specified in Section 112 of the German Civil Code (BGB) – may run a business if the minor employer is authorized by his or her legal representative and by the guardianship court. The minor employer is considered to be legally competent in regard to all the affairs of the business, and is therefore also entitled to conclude employment contracts with employees.

II. Legal prohibitions concerning the conclusion of an employment contract

1. The freedom to conclude an employment contract is restricted by certain employment prohibitions which particularly concern children and adolescents.

Child labour is defined in the Young Persons Employment Act (Jugendarbeitsschutzgesetz – JArbSchG). Under the terms of Section 2 JArbSchG, children are young people under the age of 15, and adolescents are young people above 15 and under 18.

The above law stipulates that adolescents are to be regarded as children as long as they are required to attend school. The duration of compulsory schooling depends on the laws of the individual state. This is because each federal state has

---

[97] Münchener Kommentar zum Bürgerlichen Gesetzbuch mit Nebengesetzen, 5. Aufl., 2006-2010, § 113, Rndr. 7, Schmitt

cultural sovereignty and is not treated uniformly by federal law.

Compulsory full-time education generally lasts nine school years. If a student has to repeat a year, compulsory school attendance will be automatically extended for that period.

The employment of children who are required to attend school full-time is not allowed. There are legal exceptions, as for example in the case of easy work for children aged 13 or older. Children over 13 and under 15 are allowed to work two hours a day on weekdays, provided the work is suitable for their age group and is not performed before or during their school lessons. Such tasks could be, for example, working as a paperboy, babysitting, running errands, walking dogs or tutoring schoolmates.

Children between 15 and 18 who are still of compulsory school age, may work for a maximum of four weeks per year during the school holidays.

Work experience placements in companies, undertaken by pupils during their last year at secondary school, are a kind of traineeship, and are not covered by the Young Persons Employment Act (Jugendarbeitsschutzgesetz – JArbSchG).

2. Regulations concerning employment prohibitions and restrictions are also stated in the Social Security Code (Sozialgesetzbuch – SGB).

Pursuant to Section 284 SGB III in conjunction with Section 4,18 of the Residence Act (Aufenthaltsgesetz – AufenthG), foreign workers without a work permit issued by the German Federal Employment Agency (Bundesagentur für Arbeit) may not be employed. Employers from other member countries of the EU are excluded from this ban, unless they are residents of countries that have recently become members of the EU.

3. The freedom to conclude an employment contract is not only characterized by bans and sanction – as described above – but also by legal recommendations.

Section 71,77 of the Social Security Code IX (Sozialgesetzbuch IX), obliges companies with more than 20 employees to engage severely handicapped employees up to a mandatory percentage of 5 % of their workforce. Employers can bypass this regulation by paying compensatory payment as stated in Section 77 of the Social Security Code IX (Sozialgesetzbuch IX). For each post reserved for disabled employees that remains vacant, the employer has to pay between 105.-€ and 260.- € per month and workplace.

III.   Formal requirements

III.1.   General formal provisions

The basis of every employment relationship is an employment contract, which arises from corresponding declarations of intention by the two contracting parties.

Like every other contract an employment contract can also be made informally. There are no formal requirements and the contract can be made by means of conclusive behaviour.

If an employee or employer says that "there was no employment contract", it can be taken to mean that no written contract was drawn up.

In reality, however, in most cases the parties have "de facto" entered into an employment agreement. A disadvantage of this procedure is that without any written documentation of the contents of the employment contract, a party making a legal claim may well find it extremely difficult to provide the required evidence.

If the parties conclude a temporary employment contract for a fixed term, it is only the sunset clause or time limitation that must be put down in writing. If this is omitted, the contract will be valid for an indefinite period of time (see Section 14 paragraph V and Section 21 of the Act on Part-Time Work and Fix-Term Contracts (Teilzeitbefristungsgesetz – TzBfG)). The employer has the right to raise an objection within a period of three weeks after the ending of the fixed-term contract. According to Section 16, 17 and 21 of the Act on Part-Time Work and Fix-Term Contracts (Teilzeitbefristungsgesetz – TzBfG), in this case the contract will not be prolonged and will not be automatically changed into a contract for an indefinite period.

Pursuant to Section 127 and Section 125 paragraph 2 of the German Civil Code (BGB), each of the contracting parties can make a special agreement to conclude the employment contract only in written form.

Amendments to the terms and conditions of the employment contract must be written down in order to be valid. This is called the "clause in simple written form" (einfache Schriftformklausel). Even alterations to the written form clause must be made in writing - the so-called "clause in double written form" (doppelte Schriftformklausel).

III.2. Law on the Notification of Conditions Governing an Employment Relationship – Nachweisgesetz (NachweisG)

Because an employment contract can be entered into at any time and any place, it became clear to the legislator, in the mid nineteen nineties, that the employee, for his own protection, should have a legal claim to a written documentation of the essential contents of the employment contract entered into. These considerations led to the "Law on the Notification of Conditions governing an Employment Relationship" – Nachweisgesetz (NachweisG) -.

That was an excellent way of integrating the Law of Notification of Conditions (NachwG) into the legal system, without hindering or making the informal conclusion of an employment contract more difficult.

According to the clauses of the Law of Notification of Conditions (NachwG), the employer is merely obliged to document all the essential conditions agreed on by both parties, and to give the signed paper to the employee within a month after the beginning of the employee-employer relationship.

The Law of Notification of Conditions (NachwG) defines the essential conditions of an employee-employer relationship, which are to be recorded, as follows:

-- the parties involved in the employee-employer relationship,

-- the start of the employee-employer relationship,

-- the place of work,

-- the sort of work that is due, according to the contract,

-- the remuneration for the work, to be paid by the employer,

-- the working time of the employee,

-- the amount of holiday, and

-- the terms of notice agreed on.

If, in the case of a valid contract that was originally informal, an employer contravenes his obligation – as postulated by the Law of Notification of Conditions (NachwG) - to make a written record of the above essential conditions, this does not invalidate the employment contract. The informal employment contract continues to be valid, despite the employer's offence. On the one hand, the employee can claim for a written specification of the contents of the valid informal employment contract, and this claim against the employer is actionable and enforceable before an industrial court. On the other hand, if the employer's failure to record the conditions leads to a dispute over the contents and extent of the employment contract, the employee has the benefit of some proof relief. It is then not the employee who must prove the contents and extent of the employment contract, but rather, by way of shifting the burden of proof, it is the employer who must prove that the terms of the employment contract are not those claimed by the employee.

IV. Acceptance by consensus of the employment contract

The basis of every employment relationship is an employment contract which arises from corresponding declarations of intent by the two contracting parties.

One of the contracting parties makes an offer, as in Section 145 of the German Civil Code (BGB), and declares his intent. The other party, the recipient of this declaration, then accepts the offer, as stated in Section 147 of the German Civil Code (BGB).

In order to express a valid declaration of intent, the person must be aware that he or she is entering a legal transaction ("Handlungs- und Erklärungsbewußtsein") and establishing legal relations ("Geschäftsbindungswille"). According to Section 130 paragraph 2 of the German Civil Code (BGB), it is of no consequence if the tenderer dies or becomes legally incapable after expressing a valid declaration of intent.

The declaration of intent has to reach the addressee in order to produce the desired legal effects. This is a direct consequence of Section 130 paragraph I sentence 1 of the German Civil Code (BGB), which stipulates that a declaration of will has to come into the possession either of the addressee or of a third party entitled to accept the declaration. Thereby, in ordinary circumstances, the addressee must have the opportunity to take note of the declaration of intent.

The content of the offer must be expressed clearly, so that the mere acceptance of the offer validates the contract.

The recipient must state his declaration of acceptance within a required period of time, and this statement must be received by the tenderer. According to Section 147 of the German Civil Code (BGB), the length of this period depends on whether the persons receiving the declaration of intent are present or not. If the declaration of acceptance is adopted at a later date, it qualifies as a new offer, as stated in Section 150 paragraph 1 of the German Civil Code (BGB).

Pursuant to Section 150 paragraph 2 of the German Civil Code (BGB), the same applies if the offer is only accepted in a modified version.

Guide for Romanian and German Labour Law
Basics of the Employment Relationship

V. Power of attorney and proxy

V.1. Authority of attorney and proxy

An employer concluding an employment contract can be either a natural or a legal person. In the first case, the employer himself bears all rights and responsibilities concerning the employment relationship. In the latter case, the burden lies with the person representing the legal entity, and it is this person who could incur liabilities.

The shareholders of a general partnership ("Offene Handelsgesellschaft – OHG) or of a limited commercial partnership (Kommanditgesellschaft – KG) represent the company, and their authority is required by law.

The company members, according to Section 125 paragraph 1 of the Commercial Code (Handelsgesetzbuch – HGB), usually have the sole right to represent the company legally and hence the right to conclude or to terminate employment contracts. In the case of joint power of representation, all shareholders must act together to incur liability, as stated in Section 125 paragraph 2 of the Commercial Code (Handelsgesetzbuch – HGB).

Members of a company constituted under civil law (Gesellschaft Bürgerlichen Rechts) can only represent the company as a joint proxy as laid down in Section 714 and 709 of the German Civil Code (BGB).

General partnerships ("Offene Handelsgesellschaft – OHG), for example, and limited commercial partnerships (Kommanditgesellschaft – KG), can be represented by proxies. These can be procurators, as stated in Section 48 of the Commercial Code (Handelsgesetzbuch – HGB) in conjuction with Section 164 of the German Civil Code (BGB), or authorised agents, as stated in Section 54 of the Commercial Code

(Handelsgesetzbuch – HGB). In this case the proxy represents the company by power of attorney and not by law.

V.2.   Representation with power of attorney

Within the internal relationship - between principal and proxy – it must be clearly distinguished whether or not there is in fact a proper power of attorney. Basically, no particular form is required when giving authority to a proxy, as stated in Section 167 paragraph 2 of the German Civil Code (BGB). The principal is free to determine the level of the power of attorney.

The revelation of that power of attorney of a proxy in relation to third parties while acting for the principle is a different matter.

Section 174 of the German Civil Code (BGB) refers to the situation when a proxy has to announce the termination of an employment contract. Because a letter of dismissal has to announce clearly and unambiguously who, or on whose behalf, a cancellation is being declared, means that a representative always has to be explicit. However, these requirements may be moderated in practice. A phrase like "p.p." or "per pro" - meaning "on behalf of" – next to the signature is usually acceptable.

Furthermore, the representative has to add the original power of attorney to the declaration of cancellation. If a representative fails to attach the certificate of authority, the addressee has the right to reject the cancellation immediately on these grounds. The declared cancellation then becomes invalid from the beginning, as laid down in Sec. 174 sent. 1 of the German Civil Code (BGB).

There is only one case in which it is unnecessary to attach an original certificate of authority, pursuant to Sec. 174 sent. 2 of the German Civil Code (BGB), and that is if the principal has informed the addressee expressly or conclusively about the power of attorney before the cancellation was declared. This may be understood as a case of ostensible or tolerance authority. However, it is never sufficient if the representative alone informs the addressee about the declaration of cancellation.

The special regulation of Sec. 174 sent. 2 of the German Civil Code (BGB) usually applies, for example, if the representative of the employer's company has a position which automatically allows him to conclude or cancel employment contracts. A procurator, for example, a general agent or a manager of the personnel department has power of attorney by reason of his or her individual position in a company.

The question as to whether the head of a business department, a branch manager or a simple personnel assistant is automatically endowed with the authority to declare a cancellation pursuant to Sec. 174 sent. 2 of the German Civil Code (BGB), is still a matter of juristical dispute, and has not yet been finally decided by either a German State Labour Court or the German Federal Labour Court.

It must be emphasized that the duty to attach the certificate of authority only applies to chosen representatives, but not to so-called legal or administrative representatives.

These could be, for example, the managing directors of a limited liability company (GmbH) or the members of the executive board of a stock corporation (AG). In such cases the power of attorney is a consequence of the corporate position of the representative, and the publication of his or her name in the commercial register.

V.3.   Representation without power of attorney

If an alleged representative does not de facto have power of attorney, it is a different situation than if a representative has only forgotten to show the relevant certificate of authority, as stated in Sec. 174 of the German Civil Law (BGB). The power of attorney of a representative who is only authorised to act collectively with other representatives is also invalid.

In the practical business world, it is customary for the members of the board of representatives to delegate a sub-power of attorney to each member of the board, with individual power of representation.

Taken literally, this means that all the members of the board of representatives delegate a single sub-power board. This does not come under Sec. 180 but under Sec. 174 senl. 1 of the German Civil Code.

As a consequence, if the addressee is not sure whether a proper power of attorney really exists, or whether the representative has only forgotten to hand over the certificate of authority, he would be advised to lodge a complaint on both counts – for the absence of the power of attorney and of the certificate of authority.

Chapter II

Hiring Process

I. Job Advertisment

I.1.) "invitatio ad offerendum"

A job advertisement given out by an employer does not qualify as an offer to an employee to conclude an employment contract with an appointee. It is only a so-called "invitatio ad offerendum". [98]

A job advertisement is merely an invitation to employees seeking work to offer their work capacity to this employer within the framework of the advertisement. After the applicant has responded to the advertisement, it is up to the employer to choose whether to conclude a contract or not. If the job advertisement were taken to be an offer on the part of the employer, any applicant could conclude an employment contract simply by accepting it.

I.2.) General Equal Treatment Act

The job offer must be in accordance with the principle of Equal Treatment granted under the General Act on Equal Treatment (Allgemeines Gleichbehandlungsgesetz – AGG).

The intention of the legislator was to ban discrimination on the grounds of religion, belief, disability, age and sexual orientation. The directives of the European Union, 2000/78 EG, 2000/43/EG, 2004/113/EG and 2006/54/EG have been integrated into German law. Before the General Act on Equal Treatment (Allgemeines Gleichbehandlungsgesetz – AGG) came into force on August 18th 2006, German law had already prohibited discrimination

---

[98] Palandt, 71. Auflage, 2012, § 145, Rndr.

in several single rulings. Section 611 a of the German Civil Code (Bürgerliches Gesetzbuch – BGB) banned discrimination based on sex. Applicants applying for a job in public service already had the right to equal treatment as stated in Article 33 of the German Constitution (Grundgesetz – GG) according to their personal talents, qualifications and professional achievements.

a.) According to Section 1 AGG, employed persons may not be discriminated on grounds of race, ethnic origin, sex, religious beliefs, disability, age or sexual orientation. Under the terms of Section 5 and 8 AGG there are two exceptions from this legal rule which justify unequal treatment. Discrimination against an applicant will be lawful if the difference in treatment is based on crucial requirements for carrying out the work in hand. However, this exception must be interpreted restrictively. Even for the job as a equal opportunities officer no particular sex is required.[99] As stated in Section 5 AGG an unequal treatment will be further legitimate, if disadvantages, linked to any of the reasons mentioned in Section 1 AGG, are prevented or compensated by appropriate and proportionate measures.

b.) It is important to distinguish between direct and indirect discrimination. As stated in Section 3 AGG, it is a case of direct discrimination when a person is treated worse, for any of the reasons mentioned in Section 1 AGG, than another person would have been treated in a comparable situation.

---

[99] (BAG NZA 1999,371)

Section 3 paragraph 2 AGG describes indirect discrimination, which occurs if supposedly neutral provisions disadvantage a person for any of the reasons mentioned in Section 1 AGG, compared to other people in a comparable situation.

c.) Section 11 AGG stipulated that job vacancies and conditions for the access to an employment had to be in accordance with the rulings of the General Act of Equal Treatment. On the other hand, there was no mention of any sanctions in the case of non-fulfillment. Section 15 AGG then granted compensation for material and non-material damages in the case of discrimination concerning access to an employment. An applicant does not have a right to be hired or promoted – as excluded in Section 15 paragraph 6 AGG. It was therefore impossible for the General Act of Equal Treatment to create an obligation to enter into an employment contract and hence to elude the freedom of contract.

As far as discrimination during the course of the hiring process is concerned, the applicant can demand compensation for material damages, e.g. lost profit, if the employer deliberately disregards his obligation in terms of Section 15 paragraph 1 AGG.

The applicant can demand adequate compensation for non-material damages as laid down in Section 15 paragraph 2 AGG, even if the discrimination during the hiring process was not the fault of the employer. In the case of discrimination, compensation will not exceed the average wage of three months, even if the applicant would not have been hired without any violation of the General Act of Equal Treatment. The exact amount of compensation depends on the individual case and the seriousness of the offence.

According to Section 15 paragraph 4 AGG compensation must be claimed within a period of two months. It is not necessary for the rejected applicant to demand a particular amount of compensation from the employer. The legal deadline begins when the applicant receives a negative answer from the employer, and the exact end of the period must be calculated as laid down in Section 187 ff. of the German Civil Code (Bürgerliches Gesetzbuch – BGB). If the employer does not react or refuses to pay compensation, the applicant must file a suit at the Labour Court within three months.

II.   Application

II.1.   Duties of Revelation

The pre-contractual relationship between applicant and employer is a confidential relationship between the two parties. This pre-contractual relationship, based on trust, establishes certain duties for both parties, the most important of which are mutual obligations to disclose facts, the duty of care and the duty to compensate outlay.

It is the duty of the applicant to disclose all facts which are relevant for his or her future work – truthfully and without express request. A truck driver has to reveal previous convictions for traffic offences or preliminary investigations which could ban him from driving in the near future. An accountant must disclose a previous conviction for property offences. This obligation to disclose ends when the sentence is no longer registered in the Federal Central Criminal Register or in a police clearance certificate. The period that elapses before such a registration is cancelled depends on the seriousness of the offence, but it generally takes a minimum of 5 years.

The employer, on the other hand, is also legally bound to disclose circumstances which would affect the employee and his job, like, for example, impending bankruptcy or an imminent loss of the workplace. Beyond this, it is also the employer's duty to take suitable care of the application documents of the candidate, who, in turn, is bound to the non-disclosure of data concerning the employer's company. The employer only has to reimburse the expenses of the application if he has required uncustomary application documents.

II.2. Legal consequences

If the applicant deliberately violates his or her pre-contractual duties, he or she is liable for all financial damages, being guilty of contractual negligence, also called "culpa in contrahendo," and the employer has the right to appeal against the employment contract.

III. Job Interview

III.1. Right to ask questions

The right of privacy, as stated in Article 1 and 2 of the German Constitution (Grundgesetz – GG), limited the employers former unreserved right to ask the applicant everything he wanted to know during the interview.

Nowadays, the only questions that must be answered by the applicant are those which are directly related to the future employment relationship and which are in the employer's rightful und legitimate interest. The applicant is not obliged to answer questions which would violate his personal rights and privacy.

Furthermore, he or she has the right to answer inadmissible questions with a lie. However, all information given voluntarily by the applicant must be true.

The difference between inadmissible and admissible questions is a matter of weighing up interests. We must compare the applicant's right of privacy on the one hand, with the employer's need to know as much as possible about his prospective employee on the other hand.

According to the Federal Labour Court, it is only an incorrect answer of an applicant to an employer's valid question that can justify dismissal by the employer. Employees' right to privacy increasingly curtails the right of the employer to ask questions during a job interview.

a.) For decades, employers, carrying out recruitment negotiations, had the uncontested right to ask a female applicant whether she was pregnant or not. The interests of the potential employer were predominant and the female applicant's right to privacy was put aside. The pregancy of a female employee brings financial and organisatory disadvantages to the employer, for example when the internal operating procedure has to be reorganised to protect her health interests during the pregnancy. From the early sixties until the beginning of the nineties, the right of the employer to ask a female applicant if she was pregnant or not was seen as a lawful question, even if it was clear that the employer's only intention was to avoid employing a pregnant woman.

Since the decision of the Federal Labour Court in 1992, the question as to an existing pregnancy is now regarded as discrimination on the grounds of sex, and violates Section 7 of the General Act of Equal Treatment (Allgemeines

Gleichbehandlungsgesetz – AGG).[100] It does not make any difference if the applicants are only female, or whether there are also male candidates applying for the job.

Even if the female applicant is applying for a permanent contract, and would be unable to start working because of an "employment ban" - Section 4 of the Maternity Protection Act (Mutterschutzgesetz – MuSchG) – the potential employer is not permitted to ask about a possible pregnancy. There is a statutory ban of employment for expectant mothers, if her work is connected with assembly-line work, piecework and lifting heavy goods.

If the female applicant were to answer this inadmissible question incorrrectly, there would be no negative legal consequences for her during the ensuing employment relationship.

b.) The right of employers to question applicants about physical handicaps violates their constitutional right to equal treatment, as laid down in Article 3 of the German Constitution (Grundgesetz – GG), and is regarded as discrimination on the grounds of Section 7 and 8 of the General Act of Equal Treatment (AGG). The employer is only entitled to ask about the absence of any handicaps if this is essential for the work at issue[101].

c.) As described above, the employer is only allowed to ask questions about any previous convictions on the part of the applicant if a conviction would be relevant to the work to be carried out by the future employee[102].

d.) As stated in Section 10 of the General Act of Equal Treatment (Allg. Gleichbehandlungsgesetz – AGG), the employer may legally require the candidate to state his or her age

---

[100] 1993,257 / BAG NZA 2993,848/ EuGH NZA 2001,1241
[101] BAG 1985,57 / NZA 2007,169
[102] BAG 1999,975

without discrimination only if the amount of income is dependant upon the age of the applicant.

e.) On the subject of an HIV-infection, the employer has the right to ask about an HIV-infection that has already broken out. If the applicant is only infected by the virus, the employer is entitled to ask the applicant whether the job of the infected applicant will endanger other people[103]. An HIV-infection is not classified as an illness, as stated in Section 1 of the General Act of Equal Treatment (AGG)[104].

f.) After the reunification of Germany, the highly controversial question arose as to the right of an employer - especially in the civil service - to ask an applicant about his or her former involvement with the State Security Service of the former German Democratic Republic (GDR), known as the "Stasi" in everyday language. According to BAG NZA 2003, 265, the question must be justified by a particular interest on the part of the employer[105]. This would be the case, for example, if there were a likelihood that the applicant might come in contact with his or her former victims, or with items of national security.

If a civil servant answers this question with a lie, he or she runs the risk of being punished by criminal law[106].

III.2.) Tests and medical examinations

Asking questions is only one part of the application procedure. The employer often wants to get to know the applicant better, and for this reason the future employee should make

---

[103] NZA 1988, 74
[104] EuGH NZA 2006,839
[105] BAG NZA 2003, 265
[106] BGH NJW 1999,1485

pre-employment tests and undergo medical and psychological examinations.

There are a variety of ways of reviewing the personal background and the technical skills of an applicant. Beside medical and psychological examinations, employers also request intelligence and creativity tests, assessment and graphological tests, drug screening and alcotests. The applicant has to present employers' references and bank references, and internet social networks are frequently used to get more about the applicant.

The legal admissibility of tests and examinations such as these are subject to exacting requirements. Tests for selecting personnel are only legal if the applicant is tested with regard to skills which are directly connected to the future workplace. Tests and examinations which are not workplace related and which are aimed at assessing the whole personality or the individual resilience of the applicant are inadmissible.

Legal commentators therefore demand that employers should be obliged to reveal the extent and the intent of the tests involved before they are carried out. The medical or psychological examinations of applicants, performed by fiduciary or company doctors, should only be legal if the physician is accredited and sworn to medical confidentiality.

The employer is then only informed about the overall result of the examination of the applicant, and is not entitled to know the result of individual studies and tests. The doctor is also not authorized to inform the employer about diagnoses.

In all these cases the approval of the applicant is indispensable. If the applicant is underage, the legal representatives, usually the parents, have to give their approval instead of the minor. It must be emphasised that all tests and examinations are on a voluntary basis and are not enforceable by the employer. The applicant is therefore not legally bound to consent to any tests whatsoever.

Even if the applicant agrees to a test, drug screening and alcotests are only legal if the occupation involves special risks for the applicant or for third parties, as does the job of a pilot or a truck driver, or if the employee has to handle very expensive machinery. If the employer has a reasonable suspicion that the applicant may have problems with drugs or alcohol, the employer may also require drug screening and an aloctest.

Sometimes employers use graphological reports to draw conclusions on the personality structure of the applicant from handwritten curriculum vitae. This is illegal without the express consent of the applicant. The applicant could require the destruction of the graphological report and could demand financial compensation as a consequence of the violation of his or her constitutional rights. If the applicant is applying for a job as an unskilled worker, for example, such tests are always inadmissible, because they contravene the principle of proportionality.

All applicants have the right of access to all the results of the tests and examinations, no matter whether they are accepted as an employee or not. If the applicant is turned down, he or she can refuse to allow the storage of the examination reports by the employer, can demand that the reports be destroyed, or that they be handed over to him personally.

A further way of testing an applicant is by sending him or her to an assessment centre. There the applicant's competence solving problems, his group behaviour or his ability to concentrate will be evaluated during a seminar course. The applicants are encouraged to do role playing games or to handle conflict situations. A group of applicants is observed by several assistants of the assessment centre, who evaluate their performance.

Because of the test character of an assessment centre, the applicants must consent to their participation and must be informed before attending the course about its purpose and the forseeable procedure. Otherwise it is an illegal method of testing applicants.

III.3.) Further sources of information

The submission of training certificates and employer´s references are further sources of information for the employer on his quest for more knowledge of the applicant's qualifications. The employer is legally entitled to ask the applicant's former employer about his or her behaviour and professional performance. The employer is allowed to gather information without the knowledge of the applicant or even against his or her will. However, the surrender of the complete personal file by the former employer against the will of the applicant oversteps the mark.

The applicant could then claim compensation from his former employer because of the violation of his constitutional right to privacy.

In order to obtain knowledge about the financial circumstances of an applicant, the employer may try to gain information from the credit rating agency. This company is called "Schufa" for short and collects information about all loan agreements and trade credits. The employers themselves have no legal right to request information about the appli-

Guide for Romanian and German Labour Law
Basics of the Employment Relationship

cant from the credit investigation company. The question of whether an employer is allowed to request a voluntary disclosure of this confidential information about entries in the "Schufa" files from the applicant, is highly disputed. It is generally considered inadmissible, because it means in effect that the applicant also has to reveal his or her personal circumstances and living conditions.

The right of privacy has priority over the interest of the employer to gather information about the applicant.

Even the internet, and in particular social network services, e.g. facebook or Twitter, are a popular source of information. Employees voluntarily disclose personal details about their lifestyle, which can be used legally by curious personnel managers. It is thus possible that the internet may become a kind of "job-killer".

There are no standardized recruitment procedures and tests. Hence the result and the conclusions are often not easy to understand. In 2002, the German Institute for Standardization (DIN) created a standard recruitment test (DIN 33430), which defines uniform quality criteria. Unfortunately this DIN standard has not yet become law, so it is not mandatory for the employer to use the standardized version, in spite of the fact that it would make the recruitment procedure more transparent for the applicants.

III.4.) Reimbursement of expenses and so forth

The applicant can demand a reimbursement of the interview expenses from the employer if the employer invited the applicant to the job interview und promised to repay the travelling costs.

If the employer invited the applicant without mentioning the question of compensation for outlay, the applicant can demand reimbursement according to Section 670 of the German Civil Code (BGB). The applicant can demand as much as he or she judges to have been necessary, which normally comprises travel and food expenses. If a longer journey is involved, the applicant can further demand accommodation expenses. Refundable travel costs usually refer to public means of transport.

Depending on the position offered, the applicant may also demand the refunding of a first-class ticket.

Posting a job advertisement in a newspaper does not implicate that the employer is going to reimburse the interview expenses of all applicants, in spite of having invited all interested people to apply. On closer consideration, the applicants cannot assume that an employer will reimburse all the interview expenses of an unlimited number of applicants.

If the employer wants to avoid having to refund interview expenses or to reduce his contribution to an absolute minimum, he must state this proviso when he invites the applicant to the interview.

The applicant has no right to demand compensation for the loss of remuneration from the employer he or she is applying to. But under certain circumstances the employee can claim time off work from his previous employer. As set down in Section 629 of the German Civil Code (Bürgerliches Gesetzbuch – BGB), the employee is excused from work if he or she wants, for example, to keep an appointment at the employment agency, to attend an interview with a prospective employer or to attend an assessment centre.

In addition, the employee can also demand paid leave of absence from the previous employer. However, this is only on the condition that the employer has worked under contract for an indefinite period of time, that the employment contract has already been terminated and that the employee has requested leave from his previous employer.

With reference to Section 616 of the German Civil Code (Bürgerliches Gesetzbuch – BGB), the employer only has to continue paying the employee his salary for a "not insignificant time", even if the employee needs a longer time to apply for a new job. The definition of the term "not insignificant" depends on the individual case.

Chapter III
Faults of the employment contract

I.   Causes of nullity

An employment contract may be null and void on the same grounds as all legal transactions. Basic reasons are for example legal incapacity, as specified in Section 105 of the German Civil Code (Bürgerliches Gesetzbuch – BGB) or a formal mistake.

I.1.   Section 134 of the German Civil Code (BGB)

Besides that, the employment contract may by invalid, if the content violates a prohibitive laws as laid down in Section 134 of the German Civil Code (Bürgerliches Gesetzbuch – BGB). Prohibitive laws in this context are not only every rule of law, but also clauses within union agreements or company agreements. An employment contract which, for example obliges the employee to produce counterfeited money, violates Section 146 of the German Criminal Code (Strafgesetz-buch – StGB) and is null and void. The same applies if the contracting parties agree to ignore the rulings of the Maternity Protection Act in the labour contract.

I.2.   Section 138 of the German Civil Code (BGB)

If the employment contract is immoral and contra bonos mores pursuant to Section 138 paragraph 1 of the German Civil Code (Bürgerliches Gesetzbuch – BGB), as for example when sexual intercourse is enacted on stage, the transaction is null and void.

In accordance with Section 138 paragraph 2 of the German Civil Code (Bürgerliches Gesetzbuch – BGB) the employment contract is also void in the case of profiteering.

A wage is considered to be extortionate if it is disproportionate to the work involved. The German Federal Labour Court has laid down that this is the case the wage paid to an employee is less than 2/3 of the normal wage)[107]. If this occurs, however, not the entire employment contract is null and void, but only the clauses concerning the insufficient wage, which must be replaced by the usual remuneration.

II.   Causes of rescission

The employment contract may be voidable for reasons such as error or deceit as stated in Section 119 and 123 of the German Civil Code (Bürgerliches Gesetzbuch – BGB).

---

[107] BAG NZA 2009,837

II.1. Section 119 paragraph II of the German Civil Code (BGB)

Section 119 paragraph 2 of the German Civil Code (Bürgerliches Gesetzbuch – BGB), which refers to errors concerning the essential qualities and qualifications of an employee is of special significance in labour law.

In industrial law, such essential criteria are, for example, educational background, professional qualifications, state of health or trustworthiness, all of which must have a certain permanence in order to be defined as such.

Pregnancy, for example, is not considered as an essential qualtiy, because it is only a temporary state [108], as are illnesses for short duration [109]. The essential quality or qualification must be highly relevant to the work, the employee has to do. A previous conviction for larceny, is thus highly relevant to an appointment as a cashier. The withdrawal of a driving license is crucial for a truck driver, but not for a cashier; a pregnancy is a highly relevant to work as a female dancer or mannequin.

To summarize, it may be said that all questions an employer is allowed to ask during a job interview generally refer to what are considered to be the essential qualities or qualifications of an employee.

II.2. Section 123 of the German Civil Code (BGB)

Pursuant to Section 123 paragraph 1 of the German Civil Code (Bürgerliches Gesetzbuch – BGB) the employment contract is voidable if the employee has deceived the employer. The deception may be an action or the omission of an action

---

[108] BAG NZA 1989,178
[109] BAG NZA 1974,1531

on the part of the employee. In this situation the employee's obligation to disclose personal circumstances on the one hand, and the employer's right to ask questions on the other hand, will become subjects of importance.

If the employer asks illicit questions, the employee is entitled to answer the questions with a lie. If the employer reveals the truth, he does not have the right to challenge the contract, because the employee's deception was legitimate [110].

III.   Legal consequences

According to the rules of civil law, the nullity or rescission of a contract results in a voidance starting from the very beginning of the contract.

Benefits and performances, which were exchanged by the contracting parties up to that time, have to be returned, as stated in Section 812 of the German Civil Code (Bürgerliches Gesetzbuch – BGB).

To reverse the transaction of a purchase contract, the buyer gives the bought product back and the seller gives the money back to the purchaser.

If a labour contract is null and void from the very beginning, the question arises as to how to treat the employment contract up to the time the reason of nullity or rescission became known. In industrial law, the problem is that the work already done by the employee can not be returned to him. In industrial law the impact of the nullity or the rescission depends on whether or not the employee has already started to work before the reason of nullity is known or the reason of rescission is declared.

---

[110] BGA NZA 1993,257

If the employee has not yet started to work, the nullity of the employment relationship is effective from the very beginning and is called "ex tunc". The contracting parties could demand nothing from each other.

For the eventuality that the employee has already started to work, the legislative body created a special conception, which is called a "factual employment relationship".

The time between establishing the employment contract and the discovery of the nullity or rescission of the contract, is treated as if there had been a valid labour contract between employer and employee. The avoidance is effective from this time onwards and is called "ex nunc". The declaration of avoidance is taken to be a declaration of termination of the labour contract, and dismissal provisions do not to be taken into account.

The factual employment relationship does not apply, if the employment contract is null and void, because the contract violates a prohibitive law as stated in Section 134 of the German Civil Code (Bürgerliches Gesetzbuch – BGB) or is contra bonos mores as stated in Section 138 of the German Civil Code (Bürgerliches Gesetzbuch – BGB).

The avoidance of the contract is then effective from the very beginning, that means "ex tunc". A medical doctor working as hospital physician without an approbation[111] or an employee producing counterfeit money for his employer, would both fit into this category.

---

[111] BGA NZA 2005,1409

Title III

Legal relationship – Rights and Duties of Employer and Employee

Chapter I

A significant feature of the employment relationship is that the employee is dependent on his employer to a very high degree, both personally and financially. German labor law and the German jurisdiction compensate for this subordination by defining "duties" rather than laying down "rights" when defining the roles of both parties. The principal duty of an employee is to work, and the princicipal duty of an employer is to employ and to remunerate his employee. These duties are called the "primary or basic rights" of the employee and the employer, and are followed by several "secondary obligations".

In general, the following rule applies, that the rights of the employers mirror the duties of the employees and vice versa.

I. **The rights of the employer and the corresponding duties of the employee**

I.1. **The right of the employer to organize the work – the duty of the employee to work**

a.) The employer is ultimately responsible for the company, and this overall responsibility includes the obligation to organize the workplace of the employee in accordance with the German Occupational Safety and Health Act (Arbeitsschutzgesetz - ArbSchG). The employer has to organize the working place in such a way as to ensure that the health and safety of the employee is protected at all times. He has

Guide for Romanian and German Labour Law
Basics of the Employment Relationship

also to examine the precautionary measures as regards their effectiveness, and to alter them if necessary in the interests of his employees.

b.) Corresponding to the right of the employer to organize the company and, as a consequence, the individual working place, it is also de facto his duty to provide the employee with work there. Although Section 611 BGB does not mention this explicitly, the employee is entitled to demand continuous employment from his employer.

This was not the excepted legal view in the past, but legal attitudes have changed in compliance with the German Constitution, especially with regard to human dignity and the employees right to personal development.[112] An employer can only suspend an employee under very specific circumstances, but cannot be exempted from the duty to pay him his wages.

c.) On the other hand, Section 613 BGB stipulates that the employee's main duty is to carry out his work personally, and he is not entitled to send a substitute to work in his place. It follows that if the employee cannot do his work in person because of illness, he is not obliged to provide a substitute. This is stated in Section 275 BGB and is also written into the employment contract.

I.2. The right of the employer to issue directions – the duty of the employee to follow them

The right to issue instructions gives the employer the right to specify the work expected of the employee – as has already been said in the previous chapter – concerning working time, working place and workmanship. The employee is obliged to

---

[112] BAG GS NZA 1985,702

work under the employer's authority and control and has to obey his orders.

The employment contract is not only the legal basis of the employer's right to issue instructions, but also defines the limits of this right.[113] The problem is to determine whether the employer's instructions are within the confines of the employment contract or not. If not, the employee is not obliged to follow them. The conclusion is that the contractual duty cannot be changed by the unilateral command of the employer, only by the mutual agreement of both parties of the employment contract.

If the instructions of the employer are not covered by the employment contract, the employee is entitled to refuse to obey them without any legal consequences. The employer then has the right to issue a certain kind of dismissal, called a "dismissal with the option of altered condition of employment" (Änderungskündigung), which will be explained below.

With some specific exceptions, and according to Section 106 of the Trade Regulations Act (Gewerbeordnung – GewO), the right of the employer to issue directions can be limited by the employee's constitutional rights, even if the employer's instructions are covered by the contract. [114] This means that the employee can refuse to carry out the employer's orders if he considers the work he has to perform to be incompatible with his constitutional rights.

An order from an employer is always invalid if it is purely arbitrary, unreasonable or if it violates the law. A deterioration of working conditions can always be defined as a deviation from the working contract and is basically not covered by the employer's right to issue instructions.

---

[113] BAG NZA 1990,561
[114] BAG NZA 2005, 359

In the case of an emergency, the employers managerial authority may be extended, obliging the employee to carry out
additional work beyond the limits of the employment contract, in order, for example, to avoid irreparable damage to
the company,

I.3. The supervisory rights of the employer – the personal rights of the employee

The supervision of the employee's working performance and
behavior by the employer undoubtedly violates the employee's personal rights, but in practice it is unavoidable.[115] The
employee de facto accepts the violation of his constitutional
rights when he signs the employment contract. However, this
tacit consent does not include the undeclared procurement
of information by third parties, for example by a private in-
vestigator, nor the total surveillance of the employee. The
question as to whether the supervision of the employee is still
within the framework of the statutory provisions can only be
answered by weighing up all the interests of both parties.

The rules concerning the use of monitoring cameras in public
places, such as department stores, parking lots and bank
counters, are covered by Section 6 b of the Federal Data
Protection Act (Bundesdatenschutzgesetz – BDSG). However,
this legal provision is not directly applicable to the use of
monitoring facilities in companies.

Hidden camera systems may only be used at the workplace
in order to prevent severe criminal offences. They are only allowed on a temporary basis, and only if there are no other
preventative measures available.[116] Continuous TV monitoring
is regarded as a violation of the personal rights of the em-

---

[115] BAG 07.10.1987 AP BGB § 611 Persönlichkeitsrecht Nr. 15
[116] BAG 27.03.2003 AP BetrVG 1972 § 87 Überwachung Nr. 36 = NZA 2003,1193

ployee and should be used only in a careful and unobtrusive way[117], in order to prevent the employee from feeling the pressure of constant observation and evaluation. But in security sensitive areas, such as checkout areas in shops or cashpoint areas in banks, continuous supervision of the employees may be regarded as legal.

The monitoring of telephone conversations is always illegal if the employee has no reason to doubt his right to the confidentiality of the spoken word. If, however, the monitoring occurs with the previous approval of the employee, it will not constitute a violation of his constitutional rights, provided the telephone surveillance is covered by the proportionality principle. Monitoring telephone calls for educational purposes is in the interests of the employer and is therefore legitimate.[118]

The employer is entitled to control the work desks of the employees to a certain degree, like reading files which are lying open on the desk. On the other hand he is not entitled to read memos or private notes that are not immediately visible or hidden, or to examine the contents of the waste paper basket.

The employer is not allowed to monitor his employee's entire e-mail correspondance. However, he may block certain websites, may search through and filter the employees e-mail account on the company computer and filter his or her e-mail-addresses, particularly if the employer has forbidden all private use of company equipment, such as telephone, internet or computer.

---

[117] BAG 29.06.2004 AP BetrVG 1972 § 87 Überwachung Nr. 41 = NZA 2004, 1278
[118] BAG 01.04.193 AP BGB § 611 Persönlichkeitsrecht Nr. 1

Gate controls and body searches invade the employee's privacy and are only admissable when explicitly allowed by the employee.

In this case the employment contract must include an obligatory tolerance or permission of such intensive control methods but they are only permissible if they are proportionate to the situation at hand. In the majority of cases it is sufficient to open the employee's bags. Body searches are only permitted on immediate and compelling grounds.

I.4. The right of the employer to expect loyality, and other behavioural standards

a.) The duty on the part of the employee to be loyal to his employer was long seen as the counterpart to the right of the employer to issue directions.

The jurisdiction changed this legal view. The right to issue directions gives the employer the right to specify the work expected from the employee on the basis of the employment contract, and details one of the primary obligations of the employee – the obligation to work. However, it is no longer considered necessary to append the obligation to be loyal, which is now defined as a collateral obligation. If the employee fails to follow the employer's instructions he violates his primary duty to work, which will have serious legal consequences. The breach of a collateral obligation is less severe. It is still a matter of controversy as to whether the employment relationship is purely a contractual relationship or whether the personal element should play a decisive role. The personal element of an employment relationship is of essential significance, because it creates a lasting personal relationship between employer and employee. Nowadays, the

"obligation to be loyal" is specified as a mutual consideration of interests. From the point of view of the employee, the
"duty of loyalty" means that he is mindful of the interests of
the employer. On the other hand the employer also has to
take care of the interests of his employee. The term "loyalty"
is now outdated and has been replaced by the "obligation
to consider the interests of both parties".

The more the employer can trust and rely on his employee,
the stronger is the obligation of the employee to consider the
interests of the employer.

Apart from the general obligation of loyalty, the parties, particularly those involved in ideological enterprises, are also
free to agree on a "special" obligation of loyalty, bound by
contract. These so-called "Tendenzbetriebe" are enterprises
which are not subject to employees' statutory rights, and include, for example, church organizations, political groups,
unions, or publishing houses with a particular ideology. If the
private opinion of an employee could damage the public
creditability of the ideological enterprise, it is legally possible
to limit the employee's right to freedom of expression. This
special loyalty obligation could even go so far as to affect
the personal privacy and individual lifestyle of the employee.[119]

b.) According to Section 241 paragraph 2 and Section 242
BGB, the employer can require the employee to avert damage to the employer and the enterprise. The extent of this individual responsibility finally depends of the position of the
employee in the enterprise.

c.) If an employee reports unlawful and punishable behavior
of the employer to the police or the prosecution authority,

---

[119] BAG NZA 2001,1136

this is called "whistle-blowing". So doing, the employee breaches not only his or her obligation of loyalty, but also his duty to avert damage from the company. The solution is – as it often is – to weigh up the interests of both parties. The employee fulfils his duty as a citizen when he reports his employer's unlawful behaviour to the police, and his behavior must thus be considered permissible. On the other hand, the employer should be able to trust in the loyalty of his employee. According to the German Federal Labor Court, an employee who reports his employer to the police is only within the law if this measure is appropriate to the situation.[120] According to the German Federal Constitutional Court, sanctioning an employee who reports his employer to the police in the exercise of his duties as a citizen, would violate democratic principles. Civil law consequences, such as the termination of the employment contract, can only be considered if the report was made recklessly, or with full knowledge of the falsity of the accusation.[121]

According to Section 138 of the German Criminal Law (Strafgesetzbuch – StGB), it is not acceptable for the employee to report the matter to his employer in advance in order to solve the problem internally, because if the employee is aware of a criminal offence and does not report it to the appropriate authority, he will also be subject to criminal prosecution

The situation is different when an employee becomes aware of an offence by one of his fellow employees. In this case, it is the employee's duty to inform his employer in due time be-

---

[120] BAG NZA 2007, 502
[121] BVerG NZA 2001,888

fore informing the prosecution authority, especially if the employer or the company is the aggrieved party.[122]

d.) The employee is also obliged to respect certain rules of behaviour which are not set out in the employment contract and which are internal rulings of the company, which regulate the team-work and smooth the running of the company, such as rules prohibiting smoking or drinking alcohol. Such rules of behavior are – as always – limited by the employees right of privacy and personal rights.

Questions concerning the extent to which the employee will have to face sanctions if he violates primary or collateral obligations, or only rules concerning the internal organization of the company, will be discussed at a later stage.

I.5. The right of the employer to demand confidentiality

As stated in Section 17, paragraph 1, of the German Act against Unfair Competition (Gesetz gegen Unerlaubten Wettbewerb – UWG), the betrayal of corporate secrets, such as technical know-how, lists of customers or the sources of purchased goods, is culpable. Pursuant to Section 823, paragraph 2, of the German Civil Code (BGB), the employee is liable for compensation if one or more of the following conditions apply:

The employee passes on corporate secrets to a third party for reasons of competition, for self-interest or with the intention of causing damage to the employer.

After the employment relationship has ended, the employees are required to maintain confidentiality concerning company secrets by the after-effect of the employment contract. However, this obligation should not unduly hinder the em-

---

[122] BAG NZA 2004,427

ployee from using the knowledge and qualifications acquired during his working life in his future professional life. This restriction would otherwise violate the civil right of the employee as stated in Article 12 of the German Constitution – the freedom to choose and practise one's profession.

I.6. The right of the employer to prevent competition

a.) The ban on competition for commercial agents is laid down in Section 60 et seq. of the German Commercial Code (Handelsgesetzbuch – HGB). However, the jurisdiction now acknowledge that this ban cannot be applied to all employees and all employment contracts.

A general contractual ban on supplementary or secondary employment would infringe the legal provision stated in Sections 242 and 134 of the German Civil Code (BGB), and is therefore invalid. Even a contractual arrangement (Section 311 of the German Civil Code – BGB) can cause an obligation to omit working in a secondary employment.

In the absence of a contractual stipulation, the prohibition of a second employment in order to avoid competition is covered by Section 242 of the German Civil Code – the principle of good faith - because an employee should not compete with the employer in the same branch of business.[123] Employees who wish to work in a secondary employment can be required by a contractual clause to obtain the employer's prior approval. This is known as 'reservation of permission' ("Erlaubnisvorbehalt") The employer may only withhold his permission if he has reason to expect operational impairments to his company. [124]

---

[123] BAG NZA 1991,14
[124] BAG NZA 2002,966

b.) The only legal limits that apply to the question of second-ary employment are elucidated in the Act of Working Hours (Arbeitszeitgesetz – ArbZG) and by the German Federal Holi-day Act (Bundesurlaubsgesetz – BurlG).

c.) The regulations of the German Civil Service Law (Bundesbeamtengesetz – BBG) oblige civil servants to inform their employer or their principal of any secondary employ-ment they pursue. Furthermore, they are not entitled to en-gage in any supplementary job that might in any way im-pede the performance of their professional duties, that might give rise to the suspicion of partiality or might undermine the trust and respect shown to their position as a civil servant.

d.) After the termination of an employment relationship, the employee is normally no longer bound by a general non-competition ban, which cannot be inferred from the em-ployment contract in general or stated as a post-contractual duty of loyalty. [125]

However, the parties of the employment contract may come to a mutual agreement on a contractual non-competition clause after the termination of the employment contract. This clause must avoid causing undue hardship to the employee and should not prevent him from making full use of his work-ing capacity in the future. In this particular case the regula-tions of the German Trade Act (Handelsgesetzbuch – HGB), Section 74, in regard to commercial clerks should apply to all employees, as stated in Section 110 and Section 6, para-graph 2, of the German Trade Regulation Act (Gewerbeordnung – GewO).

The agreement about the restraint of competition must be submitted in writing and accompanied by a certificate,

---

[125] BAG NZA 1999, 200

signed by the employer. Furthermore, as stated in Section 74a, paragraph 1, sentence 3, of the German Trade Act (HGB), the agreement is only valid if it does not exceed a period of two years and the employer vouchsafes to pay compensation for the restraint of competition, which is also called "waiting allowance"(Karenzentschädigung)[126]. The employee in question will receive a minimum of 50 % of his salary during this period, as stipulated in Section 74, paragraph 2, of the German Trade Act (HGB)[127]

As laid down in Section 12 of the German Vocational Training Act (Berufsbildungsgesetz – BBiG) and in the regulations of the German Trade Act (HGB) and the German Trade Regulation Act (GewO), non-competition agreements cannot be concluded with under-age employees or apprentices.

II. The duties of the employer and the corresponding rights of the employees

II.1. The duty to grant holidays

The employee`s right to annual paid leave is ensured by the German Federal Holiday Act (Bundesurlaubsgesetz – BUrlG). The length of this annual holiday is, as stated in Section 3 of the German Federal Holiday Act and in accordance with Article 7 of the EU Directive 2003/88/EG, at least 24 working days each year, excluding Sundays and public holidays.

a.) Under-age employees and disabled persons are entitled to additional vacation, as stipulated in Section 19 of the German Youth Employment Protection Act (Jugendarbeitsschutzgesetz – JArbSchG), and Section 125 of the German Social Security Code / Number IX (Sozialgesetzbuch – SGB IX). The length of the annual holiday

---

[126] BAG NZA 1994, 502
[127] BAG NZA 1995, 72

for part-time employees depends on the ratio of part-time to full-time employment. [128] Collective bargaining has achieved annual holidays of 30 working days for most employees, which adds up to six weeks' annual leave.

b.) According to Section 11 of the German Federal Holiday Act, average wages are guaranteed during annual holidays. The basis for calculation is the average wage the employee has received during the last 13 weeks before the beginning of the holiday, excluding any remuneration for overtime.

As stated in Section 13, paragraph I, of the German Federal Holiday Act, deviant regulations achieved by collective bargaining are legal, and many of them include additional holiday benefits.

c.) Pursuant to Section 4 of the German Federal Holiday Act, employees receive their full leave entitlement after a probationary period of six months, irrespective of whether the employee actually worked during that time, because for example, he was off sick.[129] Following Section 9 of the German Federal Holiday Act, sick days are not counted as part of annual leave if the employee falls ill during his or her annual holiday, provided a medical certificate has been presented.

d.) The employer has the basic right to determine the dates of his employee's vacation period, but the employee is allowed to state his or her preference. This preference must be taken into account, unless precluded either by important and urgent company operations, or, as stipulated in Section 7, paragraph 1, sentence 1, of the German Federal Holiday Act, by the preferred dates of other employees who must be given priority for social reasons.

---

[128] BAG NZA 1991, 777
[129] BAG NZA 1989,362

Guide for Romanian and German Labour Law
Basics of the Employment Relationship

An employee does not have the right to award himself leave, even if the employer has unlawfully denied him an annual holiday, thus violating his duties as an employer.[130] In this case, the employee, in order to enforce his rights, can sue his employer and apply for a temporary restraining order in accelerated proceedings.

e.) The purpose of annual leave is to maintain the employee's health by means of recreation. It is for this reason that the employee is not entitled to waive his right to minimum holiday entitlement[131] . This is also the reason why the annual holiday should be in one continuous period.

The employee is not obliged to spend his holiday in any particular way, but, as stated in Section 8 of the German Federal Holiday Act (BUrlG), he must avoid or respectively omit activities or work which are inconsistent with the recreational purpose of annual leave.

The legal consequences to the employee if he fails to comply to this obligation have been subject to controversy. Prior jurisdiction gave the employer the right to reclaim holiday remuneration on the grounds of "unjustified enrichment", as stated in Section 812 paragraph 1, sentence 2, of the German Civil Code (BGB).[132]

However, current jurisdiction only gives the employer the right to issue an injunction prohibiting the employee's unlawful activity during annual leave. In the event of a repeated infringement, and after issuing a warning notice, the employer is within his rights to terminate the employment contract because of unlawful conduct of the employee. On the other hand, according Section 3 of the German Federal Holiday

---

[130] BAG NZA 1994, 548
[131] BAG NZA 1990, 935
[132] BAG NZA 1988,607

Act (BUrlG), [133] the employer is not entitled to offset the statutory holiday pay with the employee's unlawful holiday earnings. The senate of the German Federal Labor Court, which is responsible for matters concerning leave, has interpreted the statutory rule to mean that the employee's entitlement to vacation expires if he has worked illegally during his leave.

f.) As mentioned above, the employee receives a compusory minimum annual leave of 24 working days a year, which is normally granted in one continuous period within the year of employment. Section 7, paragraph 3, sentences 2 and 3 of the German Federal Holiday Act (BUrlG) deal with an exception to this rule. If it is not possible to grant the employee holiday leave during the calender year, either for personal reasons directly associated with the employee or for operational reasons, the employee is authorized to take his annual leave during the first quarter of the next year. In this case, the employee's entitlement to annual leave expires on March 31st of the following year.

Even if the employee has been on sick leave during the previous and following year, he has the right to claim his annual holiday leave. In this particular case, the holiday entitlement remains in force beyond the expiry date of the end of the first quarter of the following year.

g.) It is basically illegal to offer payment ("paying-off") in lieu of the employee's holiday entitlement. As stipulated in Section 7, paragraph IV of the German Federal Holiday Act (BUrlG), this is only permissible if the employee cannot take his holiday leave because the employment contract was terminated during the calendar year. In this case, the legal

---

[133] BAG NZA 2002,1055

requirements concerning payment in lieu of vacation are the same as those concerning holiday leave.

The German Federal Labor Court has clarified that employees can claim payment in lieu of holiday if holiday leave could not be taken due to illness on the part of the employee. The claim still remains valid even if the employee continues to be ill after the termination of the employment contract. [134]

h.) Special types of holidays, for example are paid educational leave, unpaid leave, Sundays and bank holidays.

Paid educational leave is not granted by German Federal Labour Law, but the state law of most German states (with the exception of Bavaria, Baden-Württemberg, Saxony and Thuringia) and some union agreements provide employees with paid educational leave.

An employee may ask for unpaid leave, but cannot demand unpaid absence from work.

As stipulated in Section 9 of the German Act on Working Hours (Arbeitszeitgesetz – ArbZG), and in the German Trade Regulation Act (Gewerbeordnung – GewO), employees are basically prohibited from working on Sundays – in the period from midnight to midnight – and on public holidays. There are a variety of exemptions from the ban on working on Sundays for certain types of businesses that require more flexibility. In pursuant to Section 11 of the German Act on Working Hours (Arbeitszeitgesetz – ArbZG), employees who work on Sundays are entitled to another day of rest within a period of two weeks, and in most cases they receive an additional bonus.

Article 140 of the German Constitution (GG) prohibits employment on public holidays. Every state in Germany is enti-

---

[134] EuGH NZA 2009, 135 / BAG NZA 2009, 538

tled to declare its own public holidays, according to Article 70 et seq. of the German Constitution (Grundgesetz – GG), so the number of bank holidays differs from state to state.

Federal law has determined the following days as public holidays: German Unification Day (October 3rd), New Year's Day, Good Friday, Easter Monday, May 1st (Labour Day), Ascension Day, Whit Monday, Christmas Day (December 25th) and Boxing Day (December 26th).[135]

If the public holiday is on a weekday, the employee is entitled to the same amount of wages as he would get when working on a normal day, as stated in Section 2 of the German Continuation of Wage Payment Act (Lohnfortzahlungsgesetz EFZG), which is called the "loss-of-pay principle" (Lohnausfallprinzip).

According to Section 3 of the German Federal Holiday Act (BUrlG), if a public holiday occurs during the employee's leave, it does not count as a day of leave.

---

[135] BAG NZA 2005,882

II.2.   Duty to pay remuneration

a.)   Different types of wages

According to Section 611 of the German Civil Code (BGB), the employer`s main duty is to pay remuneration for the employee`s work and, as stated in Sections 107 and 108 of the German Trade Regulation Act (Gewerbeordnung GewO), the employer is obliged to calculate and to pay the net wage in euros and to hand over a wage slip to the employee.

In November 2013, a coalition agreement between the Christian Democratic Union (CDU), Christian Social Union (CSU) and the Social Democratic Party of Germany (SPD) established a minimum wage of 8,50 € per hour for all sectors, as from the 1st of January 2015.

The basic wage is remuneration without any wage subsidies, and can be specified either in the individual employment contract or in a collective agreement. Alternatively, if there is no such agreement, it is the wage which is usually paid for work of that kind.

The employee's remuneration can be determined according to time (time wage), whereby the employee is paid for the time he or she is working, regardless of how successful the work is. The parties of the employment contract can also agree on a piece rate, which distinguishes between time-related piecework (Zeitakkord) and money-related piecework (Geldakkord).

There are extra payments for special employment conditions such as travel and accommodation allowances, or in the case of difficult working conditions. Additional payments such as bonuses or premiums are wage components provided by the employer on a voluntary basis.

Even if the additional benefits are granted by the employer voluntarily, the employee acquires the right to these benefits if the employer has already paid them several times without any reservations. Once the right is established, the additional benefit is treated like a wage supplement covered by the employment contract.

b.) Overtime

Overtime payment is payed for working time which exceeds the regular working hours, as fixed in the employment con-tract.

In principle the employee is not obliged to work overtime. However, in the case of an emergency, the employer can oblige the employee to work overtime without asking for his consent.

The German Working Hours Act (Arbeitszeitgesetz – ArbZG) does not contain any provisions relating to overtime work. Only Section 612 of the German Civil Code (BGB) stipulates the payment of "adequate remuneration". Every hour of overtime is to be paid at least as much as an ordinary work-ing hour. The overtime bonus is usually about 25 per cent.

"On-call duty" (Bereitschaftsdienst) has to be paid for like ordinary working time. In this case the employees are obliged to stay at a particular place, determined by their employer, in order to work on call outside their regular working hours.

If the employee only has to be available and contactable at all times, but is free to choose his whereabouts (Rufbereitschaft), the on-call service is not considered to be working time, and costs the employer nothing. The employer only has to pay for the time the employee actually works af-ter being summoned to the company.

c.)   Work on Sundays and public holidays and night work

According Section 9 of the German Working Hours Act (Arbeitszeitgesetz – ArbZG), working on Sundays and public holidays in the period from midnight to midnight is essentially forbidden. Specific groups of employees are not covered by the ban on Sunday work, like law enforcement officers, ambulance personnel, firemen, hospital staff and shift workers. Even for these groups of employees, one Sunday per month has to be a non-working day.

Employees working on Sundays or public holidays are either entitled to another day of rest within a period of two weeks or they receive additional remuneration. Under certain conditions, parts of the wage subsidy are tax-free. This is intended to provide compensation for disrupting the employee's way of life and as an requital for social disadvantages.

The provisions concerning night work are stipulated in Section 2 and 6 in the German Act of Working Hours (ArbZG). Night work means regular working hours from 11 pm to 6 am or, in bakeries, from 10 pm to 5.00 am. Working for more than two hours within this time frame means that the the rest of the working hours count as night work too. The normal working period for night workers is 8 hours. Up to the age of 50 they are given a medical check-up at the employer's expense every three years. Employees over 50 are sent for a medical check-up every year.

The employee is entitled to switch to the day shift if night work affects his health or if he has to look after a child under 12 years of age or a dependent relative who is in need of his care.

d.)   Short time

Short time work is a temporary reduction of working hours and wages in response to an economic crisis.

As stipulated in Section 87 of the German Works Constitution Act (Betriebsverfassungsgesetz – BetrVG), short time can only be introduced by the employer with the approval of the works council. Restriction clauses in union agreements often allow the employer to introduce short time unilaterally. Otherwise the employer has to pay full wages, because he has fallen in default of acceptance, as stated in Section 615 of the German Civil Code (BGB).

The Employment Agency pays out short time allowances if the introduction of short time is used as a way to avoid terminating employment contracts during an economic crisis.

In accordance with Section 169 ff of the German Social Security Code III (Sozialgesetzbuch III – SGB III), short time benefits pay up to 60 – 67 % of the missing net wage. Short time is limited to 6 months, as stated in Section 177 of the German Social Security Code III (SGB III).

II.3.   Further duties

As already mentioned, the employer is obliged to give a reference to the employee. It is for the employee to decide whether he asks for a simple or a qualified reference.

According to the provisions of the General Act of Equal Treatment (Allgemeines Gleichhandlungsgesetz – AGG), any discrimination on grounds of race, sex, religion, belief or age are forbidden, and every employee can demand equal treatment.

Under the Employee Inventions Act (Arbeitnehmererfindungsgesetz - ArbnErfG), an invention made by an employee during his period of employment is to be attributed to the employer, and the employee receives appropriate remuneration according to the guidelines of the Ministry of Labour (ArbNEG).

Chapter II
Payment without work

In principle, remuneration only has to be paid if the employee has performed his work as set down in the individual employment contract.

I.   Annual Holiday, Sick Leave, Maternity

The employee is entitled to continued payment of his wages during his annual paid holiday, as stated in the German Federal Holiday Act (Bundesurlaubsgesetz), during sick leave as stated in the Act on Continued Remuneration During Illness (Entgeltfortzahlungsgesetz – EFZG) and during pregnancy and maternity, according to the Maternity Protection Act (Mutterschutzgesetz – MuSchG).

II.   Employee´s Absence of Short Duration

Section 616 of the German Civil Code (BGB) guarantees the employee continued payment of remuneration if he cannot work for a "short period of time" for "personal reasons" and if the inability to work is not the employee's fault.

This provision refers to situations in which the employee cannot be expected to work, like the death of a near relative, the unexpected illness of his child, marriage, a child's First Communion, the parents' golden wedding anniversary and so on. Two or three days within a period of six months are acceptable under this provision.

III. Default of Acceptance of the Employer

The default in acceptance is stipulated in Section 615 of the German Civil Code (BGB) and refers to cases when the employee's offer of work is not accepted by the employer. In these cases the employer is obliged to pay remuneration, regardless of whether the employer is unable or only unwilling to accept the work of his employee.

IV. Employer´s Risk

The last exception to the rule, that remuneration has only to be be paid if the employee has performed his work, depends on the question of who bears the business risk. The "theory of spheres" follows the principle that as the employer reaps the profit, he bears the business risk.

The obligation to pay remuneration is not binding if the employee cannot get to his place of work and offer his work perfomance at the location of the company, because it is the employee's reponsibility to travel to his workplace.

If the survival of the company is endangered the employee bears part of the business risk, because he has to accept reduced wages after the introduction of short time or, in the last resort, the termination of his employment contract.

Title IV

Modification , suspension and termination of the Individual employment contract

The end of an employment relationsship is a significant event for the employee, because his economic livelihood is affected. The German Labour Law offers various ways of terminating an individual employment contract.

An ordinary dismissal is still the most common way, although it is always possible to terminate the employment contract mutually by cancellation the contract. Other reasons could be retirement or rescission.

The death of the employer, the relocation of the company, a factory closure or company insolvency are not qualified as valid reasons for terminating an employment contract.

Chapter I
Termination by mutual consent

Some terminations occur as a result of mutual agreements between employer and employee, in compliance with the principle of freedom of contract. Such cancellations are unconditional and need only be drawn up in writing. The freedom to terminate the employment contract mutually by cancellation was long a highly controversial issue. Quite often the employer offers financial compensation, which induces the employee to sign the cancellation contract.

This compensation sum is later charged up against the unemployment benefits, which, in view of the labour market situation, often makes the pay-off worthless. The employment ends on a particular date without notice of termination, and is a legal method to circumvent the protection against unlawful dismissal.

Chapter II
Termination by extraordinary and ordinary dismissal

Extraordinary and ordinary dismissals are two ways of terminating the employment contract unilaterally.

I.)   Extraordinary dismissal

Extraordinary dismissals, according to Section 626 of the German Civil Code (BGB), are legally possible in cases which make it unacceptable for the parties to continue the employment relationship until the notice period has expired or, alternatively, the contractual date of expiration has been reached.

They typically apply in cases of serious misconduct or for other urgent reasons, and are only possible within two weeks of the moment when the employer finds out the decisive facts which justify the termination of the employment contract without notice.

As always, a dismissal is the last resort, and for this reason all the circumstances of the particular situation have to be taken into account.

The interests of both parties must be weighed up; on the one hand the interest of the employee to continue the employment relationship and on the other hand that of the employer to terminate the working relationship immediately.

An evaluation of the interests of the parties involved has to result in a poor prognosis for future unproblematic cooperation within the employment relationship.

If a dismissal is based on repeated misconduct on the part of the employee, it is necessary that he or she be given prior warning.

Examples of grave misconduct could be persistently refusing to work, claiming unfounded sick-leave, surfing the Internet for private purposes during work-time, pronouncing xenophobic or racist statements, committing an offence, or other criminal behavior such as misappropriation, fraud, larceny, criminal property damage or gross insult to the contractual partner. [136]

II.)   Ordinary dismissal

In cases of ordinary termination with notice, the employment relationship ends when the period of notice expires. Minimum terms of notice are laid down in Section 622 of the German Civil Code (BGB) and start off with four weeks for all employees. After 2 years of employment the notice period is extended to one month, after 5 years to two months, after 8 years to three months, after 10 years to four months and so on. However, this system of extending the term of notice does not start until the employee has reached the age of 25.

Special stipulations in an individual employment contract cannot reduce, but can also extend the period of notice of dismissal. In some cases, the term of notice required of the employee to terminate the contract is shorter than the term of notice the employer has to comply with.

---

[136] BAG NZA 2009, 779
BAG AP Nr. 73 - § 626 BGB
BAG AP Nr. 26 - § 6262 BGB

Pursuant to Section 623 of the German Civil Code (BGB), the notice of cancellation must be in writing, but does not have to adduce reasons.

Employees are protected by the German Civil Code and also by the provisions of the Act on Protection against unfair Dismissal (Kündiungsschutzgesetz – KSchG). This special act aplies only to enterprises employing more than ten full-time employees (not counting trainees and apprenctices) on a regular basis. Part-time workers with a regular working time of not more than 20 hours count as 0,5, and part-time employees with a regular working time of not more than 30 hours count as 0,75.

As laid down in Sections 1 and 23 of the Act on Protection against unfair Dismissal, employees must have completed a qualifying working period of six months without interruption, in order to be eligible for protection under this law. Smaller companies with a maximum of ten employees are exempted from the Act on Protection against unfair Dismissal.

The declaration of an ordinary termination must be socially justified and compatible. In case the Dismissal Protection Act applies there are only three justifications for dismissal which meet this criterium: Dismissal on grounds of personal capability, dismissal on grounds of conduct and termination for operational reasons.

II.1.)   Dismissal on grounds of personal capability:

This kind of termination is relevant in a situation in which the employee is unable zu fulfil the requirements of his job. It is most frequently used in connection with illness, whether highly recurrent short-term disorders, chronic disease or a protracted or long-term illness.

The Labour Court has to weigh up the competing interests of the contracting parties, such as the economic impact on the company and on work performance, the consequences for the other employees, the length of the sickness, the duration of the employment relationship, the practicability of transferring the employee to an other workplace, the size of the company and so forth.

A valid dismissal on grounds of illness requires a negative or an unfavourable medical prognosis and a situation in which the employer can no longer be expected to accept the consequences of further periods of frequent sick leave. Large companies are expected to cope with this problem more easily than smaller enterprises.

The future development of a disease is difficult to predict, except possibly by the employee. Hence the employee bears the burden of proof that he will not be sick in the future. If the employee is able to prove that he has a positive or a favourable medical prognosis, it is for the employer to prove the contrary.

II.2.) Dismissal on grounds of conduct

This termination applies to misconduct on the part of the employee, and is generally invalid without prior warning. The reasons justifying ordinary dismissal on grounds of behaviour differ from those justifying an extraordinary dismissal as regards the gravity and intensity of misconduct. Such reasons might be, for example, unauthorized leave-taking, absenteeism, or the consumption of drugs or alcohol on company premises. [137]

---

[137] BAG NZA 2004,784 and 1380; BAG NZA 2006, 98; BAG NZA 1990, 433; BAG NZA 1995, 517

The line between dismissal on grounds of personal capabilty and dismissal on grounds of conduct is often fluid and a little bit blurred. Conduct refers to individual acts commited by the employee, whereas capability and competence of an employee is associated with certain personal characteristics and skills, and are mostly unintentional.

II.3.) Termination for operational reasons

A dismissal for economic or operational reasons can be caused by an economic crisis, the introduction of new technologies, rationalization measures etc. The dismissal is justified if the economic situation has made it impossible for the employer to retain the employee any longer. Redundancy is lawful only if justified by urgent operational necessities.

The employer bears the burden of proof concering the details of the economic situation and the necessity of the dismissal. The option of reorganizing the company instead of giving notice to the employee is not subject to judical control and is considered to be a managerial decision. The Labour Court can only intervene if the the employer acts arbitrarily.[138]

A futher aspect is the necessity to select employees to be dismissed. Criteria for selecting those employees in compliance with Section 1 paragraph III of the Act of Protection against Unfair Dismissals (KschG – Kündiungsschutzgesetz) are, for example, the duration of the employment relationship, the age of the employee, his marital status, number of children, financial obligations towards family members or severe disabilties. Employees who are of particular importance to the enterprise because of their knowledge, work perform-

---

[138] BAG NZA 1996,1145

ance and professional skills, can be ignored in the selection process. The employee who would suffer most from the consequences of the dismissal must be the last to be dismissed.

III.) Special Case - Dismissal with the option of altered conditions of employement

The dismissal for alteration the employment contract is a genuine dismissal, and can be accepted, refused or accepted only under reserve by the employee.

This kind of dismissal is used by the employer to effectuate changes in the working conditions which the employee does not agree to. It is a regular dismissal combined with an offer to continue the employment relationship under new or changed conditions, according to Section 158 of the German Civil Code (BGB).

The employer's managerial authority also entitles him to change working conditions. In this case, dismissal with the option of altered conditions is not applicable. This distinction is often very difficult to determine, and depends on the kind of working conditions that are going to be changed. The more of the basic principles of the employment contract the employer intends to change, the more it is necessary to terminate the contract instead of using managerial authority.

If the employee accepts the new working conditions, the former employment contract and its condtions are terminated, and the new working conditions, usually with lower standards, take effect.

If an employee refuses the new offer, he risks loosing his job. In this case, Section 2 of the Employment Protection Act (Kündigungsschutzgesetz KSchG) offers the employee certain protection. The employee can accept the offer and an-nounce a reservation at the same time.

The Labour Court must decide whether the the employer's dismissal with the option of altered conditons was justified or not. If the dismissal is unjustified, the former employment con-tract is still valid and the employee is reinstated in his former working place with all its benefits. If not, the new working conditions apply. Either way, the working relationship contin-ues and the employee does not lose his job and his liveli-hood.

Chapter III

Other Grounds for Terminating the Employment Contract

I.   Rescission of Contract

As explained in Title II /Chapter III, an employment contract may be voidable for reasons such as error or deceit. This is stated in Sections 119 and 123 of the German Civil Code (Bürgerliches Gesetzbuch – BGB).

II.   Expiry of a period

Any fixed-term contract must be consistent with the German Act on Part-Time Work and Fixed-Term Employment (Teilzeit-befristungsgesetz TzBfG).

As laid down in Section 3 paragraph 1, the duration of fixed-term contracts must be linked with objective conditions such a particular date of expiry, the finishing of a specific task or the occurrence of a certain event.

Fixed-term contracts that have no objective grounds are lim-ited to a maximum of two years. Section 14 paragraph 4 of

the German Act of Part-Time Work and Fixed-Term Employment Contracts provides a list of objective reasons as a
guideline.

While the employment contract, including the grounds for
the limitation, can be concluded either in writing or verbally,
the limitation itself is only valid if it is written down. If not, the
employment contract, according to Section 16, is automatically concluded for an indefinite period of time. A written
version of the limitation cannot be added later.[139]

As laid down in Section 14, paragraph 3 of the Act of Part-
Time Work and Fixed-Term Employment and according to
Section 196 of the German Social Code III, if the employee is
over 52 years old and has been unemployed for 4 consecu-
tive months before concluding the fixed-term contract, the
parties involved are entitled to conclude an employment
contract for a definite period of 5 years without any objective reasons.

III.   Death of the Employee

Persuant to Sections 611, 673,675 of the German Civil Code
(BGB), the employee`s chief task is to carry out the work in
person, and he is not allowed to provide a substitute. Hence
the death of the employee terminates the employment relationship.

IV.   Voluntary Service in the Army

If the employee volunteers for a particular campaign in the
German army and stays on after it has finished, or if the military exercise lasts longer than 4 months, the employment
contract can be legally terminated.

---

[139] BAG NZA 2005,575

V.   Reaching the age limit

According to Section 36 of the German Social Code VI, the statutory retirement age is 67, provided that certain conditions are fullfilled, such as 35 years' membership in the statutory pension system. Persuant to Section 77 of the German Social Code VI, should the retirement pension be claimed prematurely, for example at the age of 63, the pension is reduced by 0,3 % a month for each month of premature retirement. The maximum reduction of an early pension is 14,4 %.

Until 1991, the statutory retirement age was 65 for men and 60 for women. The law was changed In 1992, and the age limit equalized for men and women. Employees born in 1965 and later will not receive their retirement payment before the age of 67.

According to Section 41 of the German Social Code VI, reaching the age limit is not a legitimate reason for dismissing an employee on personal grounds.

However, individual agreements between the contracting parties are frequently made. In these cases, the employment relationship expires automatically when the employee is entitled to claim his old-age pension.[140] These individual agreements are only valid if they are concluded within three years of attaining retirement age.

For security reasons, special provisions apply to employees in the aviation branch. Pilots and aviators reach retirement age at the beginning of the month of their 60th birthday.[141]

---

[140] NZA 2008,1302
[141] BAG NZA 2004,1352

Persuant to the Act of Part-time Retirement, the contracting parties of the employment relationship agree to reduce the working time to half of the previous weekly working hours.

However, the "block model" is more popular today than the above mentioned. In this model, semi-retirement is divided into two parts: the working period and so-called gardening leave. During the working period the employee works full-time, and during his "gardening leave" he receives his former full-time pay without actually working.

Whereas this form of partial retirement can also be qualified as part-time work, it is reimbursed by the Federal Employment Agency, as laid down in Section 3 paragraph 1 of the German Act of Part-time Retirement.

Chapter IV
Unlawful Reasons for Termination

I.   Transfer of the Company

In cases where a company is transferred by legal transaction (as stated in Section 613a of the German Civil Code (BGB), the employment relationships are also transferred to the new owner of the entreprise (the transferee).

Any dismissals based on the transfer of a company or parts of an company are null and void. The employment relationsship continues with the new owner and all the rights and duties arising from the former employment contract are transferred to and guaranteed by him.

A company has been transferred if the transferee continues the business while preserving its economic identity.[142]

---

[142] BAG, NZA 2004,845

The Federal Labour Court has developed certain criteria to define a company transfer. [143]

The material assets of the company such as factory buildings and movable equipment must be transferred, as well as immaterial assets like goodwill, know-how or patents. The takeover of the workforce and the acquisition of the customer base also play a decisive role, as well as the similarity of the activity of the enterprise before and after the transfer. Another important factor is whether the company's business activities will be interrupted after the transfer of the company, and if so, for how long. The new owner must keep the enterprise going, acting on his own behalf and at his own expense.

Depending on the type of company involved, some factors may be more decisive than others.

Both the former employer and the transferee have to inform all employees who are affected by the transfer about the proposed date of transfer and the reasons behind it, and also about the economic, legal and social implications for those employees. This information has be given in text form, as stated in Section 126b and Section 125 of the German Civil Code (BGB).

In accordance with Section 613a of the German Civil Code (BGB) and Article 2 paragraph 1 of the German Constitution (Grundgesetz GG), all employees whose employment contracts are to be transferred, have the right to resist the transfer and demand that they continue to be employed by the former owner. After a comprehensive briefing, either by the

---

[143] EuGH NJW 1999,1697 / BAG NZA 2003,1385

transferor or the transferee or both, the employees have four weeks in which they may refuse the transfer.

In this particular case, the employment contract continues with the transferor. He is now entitled to terminate the working contract for operational reasons, persuant to Section 1 paragraph 2 sentence 1 of the Employment Protection Act (Kündigungsschutzgesetz KSchG).

II.   Business Cessation and Company Insolvency

II.1.)   Business Cessation

Business cessation does not generally justify the termination of an employment contract. However, depending on the details of the case, the employer may have the right to terminate the employment contract for operational reasons.

II.2.)   Company Insolvency

The employer can terminate the employment contract for operational reasons before filing for bankruptcy. Thereafter, however, insolvency is no longer a legal reason for the offical insolvency receiver to terminate the employment contract by an extraordinary or ordinary dismissal. Insolvency does not exempt any of the parties from complying with the rulings of ther German Labour Law.

According to Section 108 of the German Insolvency Code, when an application has been made to open insolvency proceedings the offical insolvency receiver adopts all the rights and duties of the employer. According to Section 113 of the German Insolvency Code (Insolvenzgesetz – InsO), the receiver is only entitled to terminate the contract, with a three months period of notice, in cases where there are legitimate reasons for terminating the employment contract.

III.   Basic Military Service

Whereas voluntary service in the German army on the part of an employee can be a reason for termination, standard military conscription only leads to a suspension of the employment relationship. This also applies to annual active duty training, as stated in Section 1 of the German Act on the protection of the workplace (Arbeitsplatzschutzgesetz – ArbPlSchG).

IV.   Death of the Employer

The decease of the employer does not constitute a legal reason for terminating an employment contract. As stated in Section 1922, 1967 of the German Civil Code (BGB), the heirs assume the rights and obligations related to the employment contract. The employer status is inheritable.

However, if the work performance of the employee is adapted to fit the needs of the employer and is of a very personal nature – such as that of a nurse or a private teacher – the working contract will end with the death of the employer.

Title V

Chapter I

Freedom of Contract

Basically it is up to the parties themselves to decide with whom and under what conditions they wish to conclude an employment contract. This is called 'the freedom to conclude a contract' on the one hand and 'the freedom to draft a content of a contract' on the other hand.

This was held to be an important improvement at the beginning of the 19th century. However, it became apparent that this freedom caused such fierce competition among the employees that the overall working conditions worsened, which was only to the employers' advantage. This was an unwelcome and unfavourable development, and it led to several constraints on the conclusion of employment contracts. In particular the freedom to draft the content of a contract was limited by several industrial safety regulations. Nevertheless, freedom of contract has survived as the main idea and principle of individual labour law.

This is the incontrovertible rule concerning labour contracts with private employers. Even if an employee is seeking employment from a employer in the public sector, the employee cannot normally insist on the conclusion of a labour contract. The public sector employer is also bound by the freedom of contract and is thus obliged to make a decision - in all good conscience – as to whether to conclude a contract with that particular appointee or not.

Chapter II

Various Types of Individual Labour Contract

I.   Full-Time Contract for an indefinite Period

A full-time (open-ended) contract is the standard labour contract. Employees prefer the security of a labour contract for an indefinite period. This is because German Labour law places an employee in a very strong position, in particular as regards unfair dismissal.

Even when the economy is booming every employee has to meet the requirements of a probationary period, usually lasting 6 months, in order to get a full-time labour contract for an indefinite period of time. Nowadays, in times of economic downturn, most employees are only offered a fixed-term labour contract, even if they have completed their probation time successfully. It should be emphasized that employees nowadays are given the option of a lifelong position in a company much later than in previous times.

II.   Contract for a definite Period

According to the Act on Part-time Work and Fixed-Term Contracts (Gesetz über Teilzeitarbeit und befristete Arbeitsverträge – TzBfG) from 2001, a fixed-term contract is given either if the parties agree on a termination or finish date, or if the date of expiry depends on the purpose or nature of the work. The basic rule is laid down in Section 14 paragraph I TzBfG. The conclusion of a fixed-term contract is only valid if there is a reason which justifies the limitation.

The text of the law provides several legal reasons, but the enumeration is not exhaustive. Acceptable and justifying reasons could be, for example, a temporary demand for work in the company, the necessity to replace a former employee, to test a new employee, or if the employee is payed by a public budgetary fund.

Section 14 paragraph II TzBfG is the first exception to the principle of the foregoing rule of Section 14 paragraph I TzBfG. In this case, a fixed-term contract is valid without any justification if it is concluded for a maximum period of two years. A contract for a shorter term could be prolonged up to three times until the same maximum period has been reached.

For start-up companies, the maximum duration of such contracts can be extended from two years to four years without any justification. This regulation is intended to help newcomers establish themseves on the market without too much financial liability to their employees.

The conclusion of a fixed-term contract is always invalid if the employee has worked for the same employer before. The length of time that has lapsed since the previous employment is completely irrelevant.

If an employee is more than 52 years old and has been unemployed for more than four months – according to Section 14 paragraph 3 TzBfG - the conclusion of a contract for a fixed period of five years is valid without any objective reason to justify this time limit. If the contract has not been concluded for five years from the beginning, the employement contract can be prolonged repeatedly for a maximum of five years.

Section 4 TzBfG guarantees the principle of equal treatment of employees with fixed-term contracts and employees with contracts for an indefinite period of time. Section 17 and 18 TzBfG obliges the employer to inform employees with fixed-term contracts about vacancies in the company, in order to give them the chance of a permanent position and to strengthen their rights of information.

For the non-teaching staff at universities and colleges and for employees of large academic research facilities there are special provisions, such as the "Wissenschaftszeitvertrags-gesetz", which dates back to 2007.

An valid fixed-term contract ends, without notice or prior declaration, on the date of expiry agreed on by the parties. The employee is not entitled to claim on the basis of the Un-fair Dismissal Protection Act (Kündigungsschutzgesetz – KSchG) or any other legal provisions of German Labour Law which normally protect employees against dismissal by the employer.

If the duration of a fixed-term contract depends on the type, purpose or nature of the work – according to Section 14 paragraph II TzBfG - the date of expiry cannot be determined in advance on a particular date, because the final deadline is usually unforseeable. Section 15 paragraph 2 TzBfG stipulates that the contract expires the moment the purpose of the contract has been fulfilled. The employer has to inform the employee of the forthcoming termination in a written statement at the earliest possible date, at least two weeks before the completion of the project or the purpose will be reached.

According to Section 15 paragraph 3 TzBfG, the employer only has the right to terminate a fixed-term contract by ordinary dismissal if the parties in the employment contract have agreed upon this eventuality in the provisions of the contract.

Guide for Romanian and German Labour Law
Basics of the Employment Relationship

If the employment relationship continues after the expiry date, with the knowledge and consent of the employer, the labour contract is regarded as a contract concluded for an indefinite period of time.

The legal consequences of concluding an invalid fixed-term contract are laid out in Section 16 TzBfG. In this case the contract is regarded as an unlimited contract, and can only be cancelled in accordance with the legal rules for an ordinary or extraordinary dismissal pursuant Section §§ 620 ff. BGB and § 1 ff. KSchG.

If an employee claims that the limitation of the employment contract is invalid, the employee has to bring an action to the Labour Court within three weeks after the expiry date of the contract.

If the limitation is invalid because the labour contract was not drawn up in writing, the contract can be terminated even before the agreed time of expiry.

III.   Contract for part-time Work

Employees whose regular weekly working time is shorter than the working time of a comparable full-time employee, are working part-time.

The employees, which are compared with part-time employees are all the full-time employees working for the same company under the same or similar conditions.

Part-time agreements have become increasingly important during the last few years.

It is mainly female employees who choose this type of contract, because it meets their private and family interests at the same time as enabling them to participate in gainful employment. Working part-time gives employees more flexibility and is compatible with the new attitude towards working life, called *"downshifting"*. The employees have more time for their families, hobbies and other important aspects of their lives, without losing contact with the world of employment.

Before the Act on Part-Time and Fixed-Term Employment (Teilzeit-und Befristungsgesetz – TzBfG) came into effect in 2001, employees had no right to claim for a reduction or pro-longation of the working time that had been agreed on in the contract.

The parties bound by the labour contract were only allowed to modify their original working time agreement by mutual consent.

The new law - espcially Section 8 TzBfG - the so-called "right of part-time work", which allowed employees to shorten the working hours originally agreed on by contract, initially triggered a large-scale public debate.

In order to qualify for this new regulation, there are two conditions that must be fulfilled.

The employee must have been employed by the establishment for more than six months and the total number of employees in the company must be more than 15 (excluding apprentices). Under these conditions the employee has the right to claim for a reduction of his or her overall working hours, and also to request a new schedule for the reduced time. The employees are not obliged to give reasons for their request or to discuss their intentions with their employer.

The employee must apply for a reduction of the contractually agreed working time at least three months in advance, and must give the employer details of the required new scheduling of his or her reduced working hours.

According to Section 8 paragraph 4 of the Act on Part-Time and Fixed-Term Employment (TzBfG), the employer can only refuse the employee's request for reduced working time for *"operational reasons"*.

The term "operational reasons" is not legally defined. The reason must of course be objective. The employer cannot refuse to accept the employee's right to work part-time because of additional administrative work or other organizational tasks. Even the fact of having to engage an additional employee to compensate for the part-time absence of an employee does not qualify as an "operational reason", unless the employer can prove that no comparably trained employee is available for the company on the labour market.

According to Section 8 paragraph 3 TzBfG, the parties of the labour contract must discuss the application for reduced working time and the new time schedule involved. If they cannot come to an agreement about both items, the employer has to reject the employee's request at least one month before the proposed changes. If the employer does not reject the employee's application in an appropriate manner and within reasonable time, the working time reduction will start, as requested, in accordance with the application and according to the wishes of the employee.

If the employer rejects the request of his employee without discussing with the employee any agreements about reduction and distribution of the new time schedule the working time reduciton will not start. The employee may repeat his or her request for reduced working time, but not before two years have passed.

If the employee does not accept the employer's rejection, the employee must file a suit against the employer to the

German Labour court. If there are no "operational reasons" to support the employer's point-blank refusal, the decision of the court will comply with the employee's request and re-place the employers decision.

If the employer agrees to the requested reduction of working time and the new time schedule, the conditions of the work-ing contract will change corresponding to the new agree-ment of the parties.

Objective operational reasons could include the following: if the reduced working hours seriously disturb the working process or the organisation of the company; if they cause unacceptibly high costs for the employer, or if the safety of the employees is affected to a significant degree.

The law also grants part-time employees the right to request an extension of their agreed working time, involving a longer part-time period, or even increasing it to full-time employ-ment.

The right to reduce or to extend the working hours agreed on in the contract applies to all employees, whether they are full-time, part-time, temporary or fixed-term employees.

IV.   Contract for temporary Labour

A temporary employment agency recruits employees in order to hire them out to companies where they are regularly em-ployed as "temp workers".

A temporary employment agency which commercially hires out employees to other companies needs a special licence or permission from the authorities.

Temporary employment is regulated by the Temporary Em-ployment Act (Arbeitnehmerüberlassungsgesetz – AÜG) and is known informally as "time work" or "personal leasing".

There are two contractual relationships between these three parties, or the "triangle", as it is often referred to, meaning the temporary employment agency, the temporary employee and the company hiring the temp worker.

The temporary employee has a regular employment contract with the temporary employment agency, which can be cancelled only according to German Labour law and the German Act of Protection against Unlawful Dismissal (Kündigungsschutzgesetz KSchG). In the employment contract, the parties agree that the employee will be hired out permantly to other companies.

There is also a contractual relationship between the temporary employment agency and the company hiring the temp worker, concerning the conditions involved in the leasing of the employee.

However, there is no privity of contract between the temp worker and the company the employee is actually working for.

The temporary employee receives his wages from his contracting partner – the temporary employment agency - and not from the company where the employee is actually working. The temporary employment agency exercises the employer's rights according to the employment contract, for example in issuing a warning. Only the right of direction is transferred to the user enterprise.

If the temporary employment agency has no legal permission or has lost its licence, the contractual relationship between the employment agency and the employee is or becomes null and void.

In order to protect the temporary employee for this eventuality, Section 10 of the Temporary Employment Act (Ar-

beitnehmerüberlassungsgesetz – AÜG) stipulates an employment
contract between the employee and the company which has hired the temp worker. It is only in this particular case that the law establishes privity of contract between the temporary employee and the company he is working for.

Temporary employees very often earn less than comparable employees working for the same company, but who have signed an employment contract with the company itself. According to Section 10 of the Temporary Employment Act (Arbeitnehmerüberlassungsgesetz – AÜG), the temporary agency has to provide equal working conditions, including the amount of the employee´s wages.

On the other hand, the temporary employment agency bills the user company a higher wage per hour than the temporary employee actually receives from the temporary agency as hourly payments.

According to a collective agreement in 2008, temporary agencies are is not allowed to pay the temporary workers less than the minimum wage. This is seen as the weakst part of this kind of employment relationship.

Because of the present high unemployment rate, the number of temporary employment contracts has been increasing continuously. People seeking employment often sign labour contracts with temporary employment agencies in the hope of obtaining a permanent job in the company they are leased to. German trade unions in particular regard the increase in temporary employment as an instrument used to further rationalization, with negative effects on the whole of the working world.

Each party within this triangle has different motives. For the employee, working for a temporary agency is a way to avoid unemployment and to gain professional work experience while improving his or her prospects of getting a full-time contract for an indefinite period.

The enterprise hiring the temp worker has the advantage of flexibility, being able to adjust its personnel to its current work and order situation. Even in times of full order books, en-terprises often only increase their staff by hiring temporary employees. In difficult times, the company can cancel the contract with the temporary agency without regarding the provisions of the German Labour law. Their own core group of workers can remain intact.

If a temporary employee falls ill, sickness benefits are paid by the agency instead of the user company.

Furthermore, the the temporary agency is obliged to find a replacement for the sick worker, thus saving the company all the organizational effort involved.

V.   Contract for Marginal Employment / "mini-jobs"

The definition of marginal work is basically stipulated in sec-tion 8 of the German Social Security Act (Sozialgesetzbuch Teil 4 – SGB IV). The German law on statutory social insurance distinguishes between two kinds of marginal part-time work. On the one hand there is the "mini-jobber" who can earn up to 450.- € a month, and on the other hand the "midi-jobber", who can earn a maximum of 800.- € a month. Both types of marginal work have a different effect on income tax and on social insurance contributions.

The act mentioned above only defines the meaning of the term 'marginal work', while the working conditions and the rights and duties of the mini-jobbers and midi-jobbers are stipulated in German labour law.

According to Section 8, paragraph 1, number 1, of the German Social Security Act (Sozialgesetzbuch Teil 4 – SGB IV), if the monthly wage is 450,-- € or less, the employee is a so-called *"mini-jobber"* and excluded from paying income tax and social insurance contributions. It is only the maximum wage (450,-- € per month) that is of significance for the qualification as a "mini-job", regardless of the amount of weekly working hours. If the mini-jobber works as a marginal part-time worker for several employers, his or her total income is not allowed to amount to more than 450,-- € a month. Otherwise each employment relationship is liable to social insurance contributions and income tax payments.

Persons employed in a mini-job, with a maximum income of 450,-- € a month, are excluded from the statutory social security system. Nevertheless, the employer has to pay social security contributions for the mini-jobber. The employer pays 30 % of the wages to the statutory health insurance and to the German statutory pension insurance scheme. The employee himself pays neither statutory social security contributions nor income tax. On the other hand, the employee is not entitled to benefits from social security, in spite of the fact that his employer pays a fixed contribution into the system. This payment is considered to be a "flat-rate" contribution to the social security system in general, and is called "risk structure compensation".

According to Section 8, paragraph 1, number 2, SGB IV, persons only employed for a short period are also considered to be mini-jobbers, provided the employee only works for two months running in one year, or else for 50 days distributed over the year.

This exemption from the statutory social security system makes marginal part-time work, especially as a mini-jobber, a popular working relationship for married women and house-wives, who want to earn some extra money without paying taxes or social security contributions. Most mini-jobbers are protected by the social benefits of the employment relation-ships of their husbands.

The second kind of marginal part-time work is a so-called "midi-job", where the employee has a monthly income of be-tween 450,-- € and 800,-- €. Unlike mini-jobbers, midi-jobbers are covered by statutory social security systems. The social security contribution rate depends of the income and in-creases progressively.

At the same time German Labour law guarantees marginal workers continued wage payments of up to six weeks in the case of sick leave, 24 days' paid holiday and a Christmas bonus. The amount of the payment is proportional to that of a full time worker.

VI.   Homework / Telework

People seeking more compatibility between their work and their private lives, such as young fathers or mothers who want to spend more time with their family, or employees hoping to reduce their commuting distance, often opt for homework or telework.

This development is not being fired by employers, who are generally afraid that homeworkers and teleworkers cannot be supervised sufficiently and that data protection issues will not be dealt adequately.

Even so, the amount of teleworkers has increased during the last 10 years. Most of these employees were not originally hired as teleworkers, but worked as "normal" employees in the companies and changed later to homework or telework by mutual agreement.

Home workers enjoy the full protection of labour law and must be treated in the same way as other employees working on the premises of the company.

The first legal regulations for homework were laid down on December 20[th.] 1911 as the "Hausarbeitsgesetz".

Homework was originally a kind of wagework. The working place was and is – according to the choice of the home-worker - either his own apartment or house or any chosen place. The employer provides the requirements for production, and the home worker is paid according to the amount of items he produces. Unlike other employees, home workers are not integrated into the working organisation of the company and the employers have no managerial authority. The home worker is free to decide where, when and how much to work. Employers are obliged to pay full social security contributions for home workers.

The most popular form of homework nowadays, telework or "e-work", is a subcategory of homework. The employees work mostly in their home office using the internet, and are supported by a range of modern telecommunication devices.

Flexible or rotating telework is very widespread. This means that work is done partly on company premises and partly in the teleworker's home office. One workstation in the company can be used by several teleworkers, following a time schedule to prevent overlappig.

The classical teleworker only works at home. There is however only a small group of employees who choose this kind of homework, because of the fear of wearing, monotonous work and the risk of social isolation.

The so called "mobile teleworkers" work in different locations outside the enterprise, e.g. visiting customers at home or working in national or international satellite offices of the company.

"On site"- telework means that external consultants are working within the enterprise and are supported by the working organisation of the company. This is the only form of homework which is not completely protected by German labour law.

German Labour Law does not include any express provisions regarding telework. Several drafts have been submitted in recent years, but in the end the idea of drawing up special legal regulations has always been abandoned, because telework is only a small phenomenon within the working world. in spite of the role that it could play in helping employers to save expenses.

VII. Employment/ On-Call Work

German Labour law deals with "work on request" in Section 12 of the Act on Part-Time Work and Fixed-Term Contracts (Teilzeitbefristungsgesetz - TzBfG).

Employer and employee agree that whether the employee works or not depends on the volume of work in the company. This means that the employer only calls the employee when there is a heavy workload. Hence the working contract only regulates the basic agreement of the wage per work unit, but not necessarily the scope of the work or the length of such a working period. However, "open-ended" working hours are – even in that case - unlawful according to the German Federal Labour Court. [144]

This type of employment enables the employer to react flexibly to the work volume. It is very popular in the hotel and catering sector, especially in fast-food chains. The employees, however, have the disadvantages of an irregular and insecure income and long, irregular working hours.

Employer and employee must come to an agreement about the total daily or weekly work duration. If the agreement is missing, the employer is obliged to employ the employee for a minimum of 10 hours a week or three hours a day. Furthermore, the employer has to tell the employee at least four days in advance when he will be expected to start working. Otherwise the employee has the right to refuse to do the work.

The employer has to pay the employee for the mimimum of working hours agreed on by the parties, even he cannot employ the employee during that time.

On-call work deviates from the principle of Section 615 of the German Civil Code (Bürgerliches Gesetzbuch – BGB), which stipulates that the employer is responsible for the economic and business risks involved.

On-call employment can´t mixed up with other working time models, like shift work, emergency service or overtime.

---

[144] BAG 5 AZR 810/07 – 09.07.2008

VIII. Job-Sharing

In this employment model, the employer and several employees agree for two or more employees to share working time and one workplace. It is up to the members of the group to determine the working time of each job-sharer.

The basic form is "job-splitting". The working hours and the tasks of one full-time workplace are equally divided between the employees involved in the scheme.

Each employee has his or her own labour contract with the employer. The termination of one employment contract can thus never justify the dismissal of the other employees involved in the job-sharing group.

"Job-pairing" is a different kind of job-sharing, in which the participants and their work are dependent on each other. In this case, because the work of every member is connected to the work of the other job-sharers of the group, the sharing partners have to synchronise their work.

Unlike the basic form, the labour contracts of job-pairing group-members can only be terminated together, with one declaration of notice.

"Top-sharing" is a leadership model based on partnership. The members have equal responsibility and take important decisions together.

All types of job-sharing are, by definition, a kind of part-time work, and stipulated in Section 12 and 13 of the Act on Part-Time Work and Fixed-Term Contracts (Teilzeitbefristungsgesetz - TzBfG).

The cornerstone of job-sharing is replacement in case of illness or during vacation. If one of the job-sharers is unable to work, the other group-members are only obliged to replace the missing part if they have agreed to do so in every individual case, or if this obligation is included the employment contract.

This type of employment was initially introduced in the United States in the mid-eighties, but is seldom used in Germany.

Title VI
Jurisdiction

Chapter I
System of Labour Courts

The German jurisdiction has five jurisdictions of equal rank. These are the jurisdiction of the ordinary courts, the jurisdiction in labour matters, administrative jurisdiction, jurisdiction in social matters and the jurisdiction of the tax courts.

The German labour court system is three-tiered: The system starts with the Labour Court first instance (Arbeitsgericht), followed by the District Court (Landesarbeitsgericht) and on to the German Ferderal Labour Court (Bundesarbeitsgericht) in Erfurt.

According to Section 16 and the following section of the German Labour Court Law (Arbeitgerichtgesetz – ArbGG), the panel of the Labour Court of first instance is composed of a professional judge and two honorary judges, representing the employer and the employee respectively.

While the Labour Court of first instance and the District Labour Court - as second instance - are composed of one professional judge and two lay judges, the senates of the German Federal Labour Court consist of three professional judges and two lay judges, representing the employer and the employee respectively.

Chapter II
Organs of Judicature

I. Professional Judge

A professional judge is appointed according to the regulations of the German Judiciary Act (Deutsches Richtergesetz)
and by the Minster of Labour and Social Affairs. He must have
studied law at university and completed his studies after the
first and second State Examinations. After three years of service the professional judge is appointed for an unlimited period of time and can only be recalled under specific circumstances. He is employed by the Federal State. Persuant to
Section 42 of the German Labour Court Act
(Arbeitsgerichtsgesetz – ArbGG), a professional judge of the
Federal Court must be at least 35 years old. In courts of lower
instance the age of the labour judge is not decisive.

Persuant to Article 97 of the German Constitution
(Grundgesetz – GG), the judge is bound only by law and justice. Personal beliefs and motives may not influence his or
her verdict. In case of commiting a breach of neutrality or in
case of bias the judge can be suspended from his function.

II. Lay Judge

Lay judges are independent and not bound by instructions or
court orders. They are appointed for the term of five years by
the Minster of Labour and Social Affairs of the relevant federal state ("Land"). According to Section 21 of the German
Labour Court Law, lay judges on the bench of Labour Courts
of first instance must be at least 25 years old.

Honorary judges are supposed to have a certain insight into
problems with employment relationships. Lay Judges repre-

senting the employee are normally nominated by trade unions, whereas the employer usually sends members of the
employers' association to represent their interests in court.

A lay judge's vote carries as much weight as that of a professional judge. However, it rarely happens that the lay judges
of the Labour Court of first instance and of the District Labour
Court actually overrule the professional judge. In practice,
the lay judge is expected to represent common sense as opposed to the professionalism of a trained judge.

3.   Lawyers and other Representatives

The lawyers are also an organ of the judisdiction and they
have the same training and take the same examinations as a
professional judge. On the one hand the lawyer is the representative of his client, who can be either the employer or the
employee, and on the other hand the lawyer is an independent agent of judicature and part of the institution of legal system.

In the Labour Court of first instance the employer and the
employee can represent themselves, but in practice lawyers
usually act on behalf of their clients. Furthermore, in the Labour Court of first instance legal aid representatives from the
trade unions or representatives of employers' associations
are allowed to represent the litigants.

While representation by a lawyer is not obligatory in Labour
Courts of first instance, it is required on higher levels. According to Section 11 of the German Labour Court Act
(Arbeitgerichtsgesetz – ArbGG), representation by an attorney is mandatory in cases before the Federal Labour Court.

Chapter III
Procedural Principles

I. Venue and subject-matter jurisdiction

According to Section 48 of the German Labour Court Act (Arbeitsgerichtsgestz), the local jurisdiction of the court is determined either by the workplace of the employee or by the registered office of the employer or company. As stated in Section 2 of the German Labour Court Act (Arbeitsgerichtsgesetz), the Labour Courts have jurisdiction over all disputes arising from the employment relationship between employees and employers. Persuant to Section 2 and 2a of the German Labour Court Act (ArbGG), the Labour Courts have exclusive jurisdiction, meaning that the case cannot not be presented or heard before another court.

If a case is presented to a court that has not the competent jurisdiction, for example if an employee sues his employer for unfair dismissal before an ordinary court of law, the latter will transfer the lawsuit to the Labour Court.

II. Procedure

The proceedings in the Labour Court follow the same rules as in an ordinary court of law.

Every court hearing in the Labour Court starts with a conciliation hearing, pursuant to Section 54 of the German Labour Court Act (ArbGG). The chairman – without the lay judges - discuss the whole dispute with the parties involved, regarding the facts, the legal issues and the evidence which has been presented. The purpose of the conciliation hearing is to find a compromise.

As laid down in Section 61 paragraph 2 of the German Labour Court Act (ArbGG), the hearing must take place within two weeks of the filing of the suit. If the parties cannot agree on a settlement, the judge will determine a date for an adversarial hearing before the entire panel. Within this period the parties must make their statements of defence. The judge normally requests the conflicting parties to attend the adversarial hearing in person.

The main procedural principles are: the principle of public trial, the principle of immediacy, the principle of oral proceedings, the principle of party presentation, the principle of party disposition, the principle of judicial investigation and the principle of concentration.

Time is an important factor in labour cases. The accerlation of the proceeding is stated in Section 9 of the German Labour Court Act (ArbGG), so the deadlines for replying to statements of the opponent are shorter than in ordinary civil proceedings.

III.   Appeal

The District Labour Court, as a court of second instance, is responsible for appeals against the decisions of the Labour Court of first instance, and examines the sentences on points of law and on points of fact, while the German Federal Labour Court reviews the sentences of the District Court only on points of law.

An appeal to the District Court is possible if the grievance is valued at more than 600.- € or if permission to appeal has been given explicitly. The parties are allowed to appeal against a sentence of the District Labour Court if the dispute is of fundamental importance, or if the District Court pronounces a judgement which diverges from the majority ruling of the Federal Labour Court.

IV.   Costs

The defeated party has to pay the court fees, which are very low, pursuant to the Court Fees Act (Gerichtskostengesetz).

In the first instance, on the other hand, every party has to pay the cost of its legal representative, so that even the winning party is obliged to pay the fees of its own lawyer.

The idea behind this is to minimize the employee's risk of having to bear the costs of the employer's lawyer, which would prevent employees seeking legal help by invoking the labour court.

In the second and third instances, however, as in ordinary civil proceedings, the defeated party has to pay the court fees and the lawyers' fees of both plaintiff and defendant. If the employee cannot pay the costs of the proceedings without endangering his livelihood, he may apply for legal aid. If the other party – usually the employer – is represented by a lawyer, the employee can request to be assigned a lawyer, as stated in Section 11 a of the German Labour Court Act (ArbGG).

Chapter IV
Everyday Business at Court

As the statistics show, it is mostly employees or work councils that appeal to the Labour Court, and more than one third of the disputes between employees and employers are settled in the consiliation hearing. The most frequent cases are claims against unfair dismissal, claims for compensation after dismissal and disputes about employment references.

I.   Indemnity

In cases of unfair dismissal the conciliation hearing very often ends with a severance payment.

The main subject of controversy is the amount the employer has to pay his former employee. The last monthly wage and the duration of employment have a determining influence on the level of indemnity. There is a rule of thumb for calculating the amount due : the plaintiff can claim half of his last gross monthly wage per service year.

With the mediation of the Labour Court, the compensation settlement often combines different issues to soften the impact of the employee's job loss. The parties might, for example, change a termination without notice into a termination with notice, in order to forestall a reduction in his unemployment benefits, and embellish the settlement with a favourable reference. Employers often demand a non-disclosure agreement, in order to prevent the content of the settlement from being known within the company.

Guide for Romanian and German Labour Law
Basics of the Employment Relationship

II. Employment References

Every employee has the right to ask for an employment certificate, which must be issued on the day when the contract is terminated.

A distinction is made between an simple reference, which refers only to the type and duration of the employee's activity in the company, and a qualified reference, which also contains details of performance and conduct.

An employer is duty-bound to provide a job reference, but on other hand the employee has no right to demand particular wording in his reference. The content of the job reference must be genuine and favourable.

Certain expressions within a reference often give rise to suspicion, implying a secret code or language behind apparently favourable wording. Hence proceedings to rectify job references are part of everyday business at the Labour Court. The following are examples of adjectives that can be used to express approval of a employee's work performance: "exceptional, outstanding, superior". "Dedicated and intelligent," for example, can be used to describe his character .The following phrases, *for example*, are clearly ambigious: *"You will be lucky to get him to work for you"* or " *"He was attentive to details, independent and flexible"*.

The omission of a concluding sentence in the employer`s reference, saying, for example, that his former employer would be pleased to reemploy him, or the lack of a recommendation to any future employers, are interpreted in the light of this secret code and are everyday issues at Labour Courts. It goes without saying that employers deny the existence of any such code language in job references.

Private Notes